The Ghostwriting Advantage

How to Get Your Book Written Without Writing It Yourself

Richard Lowe

The Writing King

Your Story Has the Power to Change Lives

The Ghostwriting Advantage: How to Get Your Book Written Without Writing It Yourself

Copyright © 2026 by Richard G Lowe

Table of Contents

See books by Richard Lowe at

https://masterofworlds.com

Get free publishing insights and industry updates at

https://thewritingking.substack.com

For ghostwriting and book coaching services see

https://thewritingking.com

Preface

Before I typed a single word as a professional ghostwriter, I was a photographer, specifically of dancers. For nearly a decade, I immersed myself in the world of movement, color, and performance. Every frame I captured told a story, and it taught me to look beyond the surface. I wasn't just photographing dancers; I was documenting passion, culture, and identity.

That journey led to annual birthday parties where 100 to 260 dancers would gather to celebrate life, friendship, and art. One year, I rented a pirate shop. Another time, I booked a town hall and brought in live performers and ethnic catering. These weren't just parties; they were immersive storytelling experiences, each one a living metaphor for the narrative arcs I would later help clients shape in their books.

One of my closest photography subjects was Marjhani, a bold and wildly creative dancer with a bone through her nose and tattoos that once made my conservative side shudder. We became friends. And through her and others in the community, I learned to embrace diversity of expression. I also realized something deeply important: everyone, no matter how unconventional, has a story that deserves to be told.

Those early experiences laid the foundation for everything I do now. I don't just ghostwrite; I extract emotion, honor identity, and illuminate meaning. And if you've ever wondered whether your story is "too much," "too weird," or "too ordinary," I'm here to tell you it's not. It's yours. And that makes it worth telling.

This book exists because of an unexpected journey — a journey that started in a server room and ended with a pen in my hand and stories in my heart.

For over three decades, I was deep in the corporate world. I worked as Director of Computer Operations at Trader Joe's, where I oversaw massive technology systems, disaster recovery, cybersecurity, and a 5,000-computer infrastructure. I was the guy who got called on Christmas Eve, on my birthday, even while my wife lay dying, because that was the job. It was high pressure, high responsibility, and high burnout.

But somewhere in all those years of spreadsheets and servers, I held onto something more personal, writing. It wasn't a job. It was a calling. At 17, I interviewed my grandfather about his time in World War II and wrote a small book about his capture during the Bataan Death March. That was my first taste of real storytelling.

So, after decades in tech, I walked away. I moved to Florida and took a job with a ghostwriting firm. The pay was dismal. The workload was overwhelming. And the message from my boss was crystal clear: "You'll never make it on your own."

Three days after I quit, I had $25,000 in ghostwriting contracts. I never looked back.

Since then, I've written or ghostwritten over 100 books; some for coaches, some for CEOs, and some for people who simply needed to leave behind a legacy. I've worked on memoirs, business books, science fiction, young adult novels, even a book about how to avoid online dangers for teens. I've turned quiet professionals into confident authors, helped introverts find their public voice, and watched clients grow their businesses, credibility, and confidence through the books we built together.

I've also said "no" to jobs that could've gotten me killed; like the FBI informant who wanted to name mafia members in his memoir. I've worked with dancers, rock stars, tech executives, billionaires, and war survivors. I've danced at parties with hundreds of friends, photographed 1,200 performances, and sat quietly across from clients breaking down as they finally told the truth they'd held in for decades.

Why am I telling you all this?

Because ghostwriting is personal.

This isn't just a book about ghostwriting. It's a field guide for business leaders, aspiring authors, and anyone who's wondered:

"Can a book really change my life?"

The answer is yes. If you treat your book like a business decision — not just a bucket list item — it can open doors, generate revenue, and build a brand that outlasts trends and algorithms. I've seen it happen. I've built the systems. I've studied the ROI. I've been the guide behind the curtain for clients who went from anonymous to unforgettable.

This book will show you how it all works: how to find the right ghostwriter, what a good book can do for your brand or business, and what the process really looks like behind the scenes. It's honest, detailed, and a little bit personal.

Because this isn't theory. It's real. And you deserve to know how it works.

Whether you're here to share your expertise, grow your platform, leave a legacy, or finally stop talking about your book and start doing something about it; you're in the right place.

If you're ready to find out how, keep reading.

Introduction

I walked into that meeting completely prepared, years of experience, great results, total confidence. The client was nodding along, engaged, asking all the right questions. Everything pointed to a yes.

Then, near the end of the conversation, they casually said, "We've also been reading her book, and it aligns with what we've been looking for."

No drama. No pushback. Just a quiet shift in trust.

I left still optimistic. But a few days later, I got the email: they'd gone with the other consultant.

Because of a book.

"I guess I don't need to wonder anymore," I thought.

It wasn't about talent. I had that. It came down to perception. Her book gave her the edge.

She had a book. Her ideas had already made their way into their minds before she even walked into the room. The book did the talking long before she did.

So, here's the real question: Can you afford to let someone else be the expert in your field — because they published first?

You've carried the idea for years. Maybe you've even stayed up late jotting thoughts on napkins or typing frantically into your notes app. You tell yourself this is it. You've waited long enough; it's finally time to get your book written.

You lean back, picturing your name on the cover, smiling. You see people reading your words, nodding in agreement, quoting you in meetings, on social media, even in magazines.

You know for a fact that your book will get you into rooms you've never been in, attract high-value clients, and establish you as the go-to expert.

But life has a way of throwing curveballs. For me, the dream of becoming a writer started early, but real life got in the way. I had to move out of the house when I was 19, work multiple jobs, go to college, raise a family, and get certified in various technical areas. This delayed my writing career until I was 55.

Occasionally, you sit down to write, staring at a blank page, and suddenly you're interrupted by your kids, the cat, or the ever-present demands of social media.

Maybe you write a few pages, but then you second-guess them. You go back, tweak a sentence, delete a paragraph. Another day passes. Then a week. Then a year.

Your book is still an idea floating around in your head.

If this sounds familiar, then you're in good company. Writing a book takes more effort than carving out a few hours here and there. If it were that easy, people would bang out bestsellers on every long plane flight or road trip.

The real challenge is understanding how to take those ideas from your head, structure them in a way that makes sense, and finish writing a paragraph, then a page, and then a chapter, until, finally, the book is done.

That's one reason many people who start writing a book never finish. It's not about writing harder — it's about writing smarter. And that's exactly what this book is about.

Your Book Is More Than a Book: It's Your Brand, Business, and Legacy

One of the first clients I ever worked with was a woman named Doris. Every morning since she was a little girl, when she woke up, she wrote down her dreams. Reams of paper, decades worth. She came to me with thousands of pages and asked if I could turn them into a novel.

I dove in. Within a year, she held the finished book in her hands. And when she did, she looked up at me with tears running and said: "This feels almost like when I held my first-born child in my hands a few minutes after she was born."

That's what a book can be. Not a marketing asset. Not a credibility signal. Something that matters. A life's work made real.

But here's what most professionals don't realize: a book works for you in ways nothing else does. It's in the room before you are. It answers questions clients haven't asked yet. It establishes authority before you've said a word. The consultant who loses the deal to someone else's book knows this feeling. The speaker who gets passed over for the author knows it too.

If you're a coach, consultant, entrepreneur, or business leader, your book isn't a milestone — it's a multiplier. It keeps working long after launch day: fueling speaking gigs, building trust with clients before you've ever spoken, turning your expertise into something people can hold.

But your book does nothing for you if it stays stuck in your head. This is where most people get tripped up. They know they need a book. They want to write it. But somehow, life always gets in the way.

What a Ghostwriter Actually Does

Every client I've worked with has said some version of the same thing on our first call. Usually it comes out as: "I've been meaning to do this for years." Sometimes it's "I have all the ideas, I just can't seem to get them down." Occasionally it's "I actually started it — there's a file somewhere on my computer."

They're not lazy. They're not disorganized. Most of them have built businesses, led teams, shipped products. They're capable of hard things. But writing a book is a different kind of hard — not because it requires extraordinary talent, but because it's entirely self-directed, entirely self-motivated, and entirely forgettable the moment a client calls or a deadline lands.

A ghostwriter changes that equation. Not by writing for you — by working with you. By asking the questions that pull the book out of your head. By turning a two-hour conversation into a chapter, and your chapters into a book that sounds like you at your most articulate. I've done it over a hundred times. The voice on the page is always the client's. My job is to make sure it finally gets there.

Your book isn't words on a page, it's a message, a tool, a step toward bigger opportunities. Maybe it's a way to attract more clients, open doors to speaking engagements, or position yourself as the go-to expert in your field. Or perhaps it's a deeply personal project, a way to share your journey, your lessons, and your legacy.

Whatever your reason, getting your book written is the difference between dreaming about it and making it real.

I typically talk to several people every week about the books that they've dreamed of for years. For an hour, we discuss how much it means to them to tell people their message and explain how they got to where they are. Sometimes, I give them a few moments as they choke back tears about their frustration that their book is not finished.

I once worked with a business coach who had been 'thinking' about writing a book for five years. Every time we talked, he said the timing wasn't right. Then, one day, a competitor published a book on the same topic, and he lost a major opportunity. That's when he called me. Within six months, his book was done, and he was being invited to podcasts and conferences as an authority.

Waiting for the perfect time to write your book? It never comes. Life doesn't slow down long enough to hand you an empty calendar. The perfect time is when you decide it's important enough.

> Every day you wait, that's another day that your book isn't out there, working for you.
>
> Hiring a ghostwriter isn't about taking shortcuts. It's about making sure your book gets written and written well.

The difference between those who have published books and those who haven't has nothing to do with talent, knowledge, or even the size of their bank account. It's action. Hiring a ghostwriter is the best way to act without putting everything else in your life on hold.

Your book becomes a silent salesperson, a 24/7 credibility engine, and a magnet for opportunity. It positions you as a go-to expert, making it easier to land speaking gigs, earn media attention, and build trust with clients before you ever get on a call. You won't always need to chase leads. Many will come to you.

What to Expect from This Book

There are at least two kinds of people who hire ghostwriters.

The first type knows they want a book but has no idea where to start — too many ideas, no confidence in their writing, or simply no time. The second has tried writing and gotten stuck, perhaps even completed a rough draft that went nowhere, and now needs someone to help them transform it into something great.

No matter which category you fall into, this book will guide you through the ghostwriting process.

The right ghostwriter doesn't write — they capture your voice, your stories, and your message as if you put every word down yourself. A great one asks the right questions and digs deeper until the book sounds unmistakably like you. I'll walk you through exactly what happens after you hire a ghostwriter, with no surprises and no confusion. And while ghostwriting isn't cheap, a poorly written book costs far more in lost credibility and missed opportunities.

My purpose is not to teach you about ghostwriting. I will show you how to get your book done the right way.

> If you get this right, with the right help from a ghostwriter, your book won't be an idea anymore.

It will become real.

In the next chapter, we'll explore why sharing your story can transform your career, your brand, and your legacy, and what you're leaving on the table if you don't.

Why Your Story Matters

Your story isn't a list of past events, it's your greatest asset. It's how people remember you, why they trust you, and why they want to work with you.

But too often, we downplay our own experiences. We tell ourselves it's our journey, never stopping to realize how much it could impact others if we shared it.

Your story is powerful, and when shared in the right way, it can unlock doors that you never thought possible. The truth is no one else can tell your story like you can. It's unique to you, and it holds the potential to connect with people, inspire change, and leave a lasting impact. So, how do you harness that power? The first step is recognizing that your story has value, value that can transcend the page and drive your success.

I sat across from Elena, a leadership coach who had helped dozens of executives' land promotions and negotiate better deals. Yet, when we talked about public recognition, she sighed and pushed her coffee aside. "I don't get it," she said. "I see these other coaches, some with half my experience, getting booked for major events. They're not better than me. But they have books. And I don't."

Elena paused for a moment. "I guess that's what I'm missing, isn't it?" she finally admitted, shaking her head.

You Have a Story. But Does the World Know It?

Michael was the person people turned to for advice. He had the experience, the results, and the trust of his clients. But then he'd see someone else, someone with half his expertise, getting invited to the big conferences.

"Why them and not me?"

It wasn't that they were better. It wasn't that they knew more. They had one thing he didn't.

A book.

Michael told himself, "I'll get to it someday." But whenever he tried to start, the same thoughts crept in: Where do I even begin? What if it's not good enough? What if no one cares?

So, he put it off.

And while he hesitated, others took the spotlight.

Why Your Story Matters More Than You Think

If you're a coach, entrepreneur, or expert, your story is your most valuable asset.

It's what makes people trust you and what causes clients to choose you instead of the competition. It's what turns you from another professional into the go-to authority.

> *People often ask me how I became a ghostwriter. I tell them the story of my grandfather, and how I wanted to get to know him. One day I sat down and began asking questions. Turns out he was a World War II veteran and hero, a cook on a ship on the Yangzi River patrol. He was captured by the Japanese on Corregidor, marched across Bataan with thousands of other soldiers, and finally spent four years in the Japanese POW camp. I wrote a short book, which we never published, and this gave me the inspiration to become a writer, albeit many years later.*

Your book isn't a project, it's a statement.

Think about the brands you admire. What makes them unforgettable? It's not their logo; it's the connection they create.

A book works the same way. It's not pages and ink. It's something that stays with people, something they can pass along, something that shapes how they see you. Something far more powerful than any LinkedIn post or website ever could.

People don't buy iPhones; they buy into Apple's story.

Every product launch is more than an update, it's an event. Every ad isn't about a gadget, it's about belonging.

That's what a great story does. And a book can do the same for you.

The most influential leaders don't teach; they tell stories.

Here's the truth: your story matters.

But too many people dismiss their own experiences. They assume their journey is "average" or that "no one would care." They think a book requires some Hollywood-level success story.

It doesn't.

> The most powerful books aren't about perfection. They're about connection.

People don't want to read about a perfect expert who has never failed. They want to read about someone who has been where they are and found a way to move forward.

Tom ran a business that, on paper, was thriving. But when he sat across from me, he looked tired. 'Who's going to care about my story?' he asked. 'I don't have some big dramatic success - a lot of near-misses and late nights.' He hesitated before adding, 'Honestly, I almost walked away from it all last year.' That's where the real story was, not in the numbers, but in the choices he had to make. The deal that saved his company, the burnout that nearly broke him, and the small wins that kept him going. The parts he thought were too boring to matter? That's exactly what his readers needed to hear.

What's Stopping You from Writing Your Book?

If writing a book creates such significant opportunities, why do so many professionals put it off?

It's not about expertise; you already have that. It's about time, doubt, and not knowing where to begin.

Maybe you keep telling yourself you'll start "someday," but between running a business, managing clients, and handling daily tasks, that day never comes. Maybe the thought of structuring an entire book feels overwhelming. Or maybe you've tried before, but it didn't turn out how you imagined.

Meanwhile, as you wait, others take the stage.

For some, the biggest hurdle is cost. Hiring a ghostwriter feels like an expense, but it's an investment, one that builds credibility and pays dividends in speaking engagements, client trust, and authority in your industry.

This is where most people get stuck. They know a book would change their business, career, or legacy, but the process seems too big, too complicated, too time-consuming, and too expensive. It's overwhelming for them.

So, they put it off.

And in the meantime, someone else writes the book that should have been yours.

This isn't about writing a book, it's about staying ahead.

Because if you don't tell your story, someone else will tell theirs. And they'll be the person getting the attention, the credibility, and the opportunities that could have been yours.

The Guide: How a Ghostwriter Helps You Finally Get It Done

Stuck? You don't have to do this alone.

You don't need to drop everything for months or stress over every sentence.

That's where a ghostwriter comes in.

A ghostwriter doesn't write your book, they bring your voice to life. They take your stories, your lessons, your insights, and shape them into something real. You don't have to struggle through drafts or wonder if your writing is "good enough." Instead of spending hundreds of hours second-guessing yourself, you spend a few focused sessions sharing your ideas. While you're running your business, your ghostwriter is crafting a book that sounds like you and works for you.

That's what Michael did.

He stopped putting off his book. He hired a ghostwriter, who helped him organize his knowledge, shape his ideas, and bring his personality onto the page. Within months, he had a polished, professionally written book in his hands.

The book launched, and the impact was immediate. A week later, a company he had been chasing for years reached out, not because of a cold pitch, but because they had read his book. Instead of fighting to prove himself, he was now getting invitations to speak at industry events. His book wasn't a credibility boost, it was the key that unlocked doors he never thought possible.

That's what happens when your expertise is in people's hands before you even enter the room.

The Real Cost of Waiting

What's stopping you from doing the same?

It's not that they're more qualified, it's that they took action.

Every time you put off writing your book, someone with less experience than you steps forward instead.

They're the ones getting booked for the big conferences. They're the ones journalists reach out to for expert insights. They're the ones landing clients before you even have a chance to introduce yourself.

The Business Case for Writing a Book (And Why Hiring a Ghostwriter Pays Off)

When Alex first decided to write a book, it wasn't about sales. It was legacy. He had spent two decades consulting Fortune 500 companies and wanted to capture his hard-won insights in a way that could outlive his PowerPoint slides. He also knew he didn't have the time, or the writing chops, to do it alone.

So, he hired a ghostwriter. Three years later, Alex found himself booked solid, not with consulting gigs, but keynote appearances where his book became the introduction. One client even told him, "We chose you because your book spoke our language before we ever met." He didn't write it himself, but he owned every word. And the return? Nearly $400,000 in new business within 18 months.

Alex's story isn't unusual. A 2024 study of over 300 business authors — conducted by Amplify Publishing Group, Gotham Ghostwriters, and Thought Leadership Leverage — found that for books published at least six months, the median ROI was $2.56 for every dollar spent. Ghostwritten books did considerably better: a median gross profit of $43,250 even after accounting for the cost of the ghostwriter (A Comprehensive Study of Business Book ROI, p. 24–25).

The same study found that ghostwritten books generated a median revenue of $92,500 — nearly four times the overall median. And 96% of authors who used ghostwriters reported being satisfied with the experience, the highest satisfaction rate of any service measured in the study. When those books were also paired with a clear revenue strategy, results climbed further: authors with a strong plan brought in $96,506 compared to $28,500 for those who simply published and hoped for the best (p. 25).

Why Ghostwritten Books Often Outperform DIY Efforts

While writing your own book sounds like the honest path, it rarely pays off as well. The study found the median author spent ten months writing their book — twelve months for those with traditional publishers. That's nearly a year of divided attention, pulling focus from the income-generating work that keeps a business running.

Meanwhile, ghostwritten books allow executives to stay focused on their business while the writing happens in the background. Authors who outsourced the writing process still achieved deeply personal and authentic outcomes, because great ghostwriters don't replace your voice. They refine it. And they bring structure, pacing, and storytelling mastery that most business leaders simply don't have time to learn.

It's Not About Book Sales. It's About What the Book Unlocks

Here's what most first-time authors misunderstand: Book sales alone aren't the main path to profit.

Median sales figures tell the real story: around 700 copies if self-published, 1,600 through a hybrid publisher, and 4,600 through traditional publishing (A Comprehensive Study of Business Book ROI, p. 11). Most authors sold far fewer than they expected. But the ones who achieved their goals — more clients, more speaking gigs, more credibility — often did it with modest sales numbers.

But the most successful authors don't rely on sales. They use the book as a marketing tool, a credibility multiplier that opens doors to new clients, bigger deals, and high-trust opportunities. Speaking engagements, enterprise sales, online courses, brand partnerships, these are the real revenue streams that a ghostwritten book unlocks.

The Tangible and Intangible ROI

The median business book generated $11,350 in gross profit, and 64% of books earned a positive return. Ghostwritten books cleared $43,250 in median gross profit even after expenses. The real money, though, came from what the book made possible: among authors who saw revenue increases, speeches generated a median of

$30,000, consulting $50,000, and workshops $40,000. On the credibility side, 68% of authors reported being seen as more credible by clients and peers, 90% saw some form of meaningful nonmonetary benefit, and 18% generated more than $250,000 in total revenue from a single book (A Comprehensive Study of Business Book ROI, p. 19, 21–25).

But beyond money, the intangible value is huge: stronger personal brand, media features, and lasting authority in your industry.

Citations

Primary source: A Comprehensive Study of Business Book ROI, conducted by Amplify Publishing Group, Gotham Ghostwriters, Smith Publicity, and Thought Leadership Leverage; research by Josh Bernoff, Bill Sherman, and Dr. AJ Marsden; published 2024. Available at AuthorROI.com.

Speed, Cost, or Quality — Choose Two

Every book project faces a familiar balancing act: time, quality, and cost. This dynamic is often referred to as the Project Management Triangle. Whether you're writing the book yourself or hiring a ghostwriter, these three forces will shape your experience. Understanding how they interact is key to setting smart expectations.

Here's the truth: you can't have all three. If you prioritize one, you'll almost certainly compromise on at least one of the others. That's just how it works.

Time: The One Thing You Can't Get Back

Every writer or client embarking on a book project is facing a time constraint. Whether you have a tight deadline for publication, a launch date you're aiming for, or simply a personal timeline you want to adhere to, time is always a factor in the writing process.

Here's the truth: writing a book isn't quick or easy. It takes real effort and patience. It takes time to research, time to write, time to revise, and time to get feedback. The idea of "fast" writing, where you churn out a book in a matter of weeks, often doesn't align with the quality that you may want to achieve. A quick turnaround often means cutting corners on research and manuscript refinement, which directly impacts quality.

I once worked with a client who needed his book done quickly, in three months. It was a complex project, filled with his personal experiences and deep insights into the subject. To meet his deadline, I needed to focus almost entirely on his book. I had to slow down other contracts, decline new business, and scale back marketing. He understood the tradeoffs and agreed to pay double my normal rate to make it happen. I finished the book on time and on budget.

When you're working with a ghostwriter, time becomes especially critical. You might want to finish the project quickly, but rushing them often means you're not getting the most thoughtful, strategic work in return. I get it, waiting sucks. You want it done yesterday. But speed has a cost, and trust me, I've seen how that plays out.

Quality: The Heart of the Book

Quality is the standard of excellence that any serious writer or client wants for their book. This is the polished product, the book that reflects your ideas with depth, emotional connection, and the perfect balance of structure and storytelling. Quality in book writing means ensuring that the writing is engaging, original, and speaks to the reader's emotions. It means that your message resonates and leaves an impact.

However, achieving high quality takes time and investment. Good writing isn't accidental, it's a craft that demands editing, revision, and refinement. If you aim for quality, it can take weeks, months, or even years to get your book right.

If you're short on time, quality is the first thing to suffer. For instance, a rushed ghostwriting process may lead to a book that feels formulaic or disconnected. It might not capture your voice authentically or tell your story in the way you envisioned. A great book requires time for feedback, revisions, and careful attention to detail.

Cost is an essential consideration for any book project, and it's often the most sensitive of the three factors. If you have a limited budget, you may have to make hard decisions about the amount of time and quality you can afford to invest. Ghostwriters, editors, and publishing services don't come cheaply, especially if you want to ensure that you get the best results. But cost also plays a role in how much time can be dedicated to the project and the level of quality you can achieve.

For instance, if you have a tight budget, you may have to cut back on the time allocated for editing or the depth of research included. This might mean sacrificing detail, accuracy, or the polished style of a higher-end project. Alternatively, a higher cost might allow you to hire a skilled ghostwriter who can dedicate more time to creating a masterpiece, but it also means that you may face a larger financial investment.

Balancing cost, time, and quality means knowing your priorities. If you want the best possible book, you'll need to invest in the right resources, whether that's a more experienced ghostwriter, more rounds of revisions, or the time to create a professional marketing strategy. However, if your budget is tight, you may need to adjust your timeline or the depth of your project.

The Trade-Offs: Time, Quality, and Cost in the Real World

Let's apply this triangle to real-world book writing and ghostwriting projects.

Scenario 1: Fast and Cheap

Say you're rushing to publish because you have a business launch coming up. You hire a ghostwriter, but to keep costs down, you prioritize speed over depth. The book gets done fast, but at what cost? The writing might feel rushed, some key details could be missing, and it may not fully sound like you. That's the trade-off.

> Want it fast and cheap? That's like expecting a five-star meal from a gas station. Sure, you'll get something, but it won't be what you hoped for.

You get your book fast, but the quality may suffer, and you risk publishing something that won't engage readers the way you hope.

Scenario 2: High Quality and High Cost

Now, imagine you're willing to invest significant resources into your book. You hire a highly experienced ghostwriter, work with professional editors, and spend time on feedback and revisions. This will take more time and cost more money, but the result will likely be a book that's polished, well-written, and engaging. It may take longer to get the finished product, but the final book will reflect your brand and vision, and it will connect deeply with your readers. However, if you don't have the budget, you may have to delay the project or adjust your expectations on quality.

Scenario 3: Tight Timeline and Cost Constraints

If you're trying to finish a book in a short period and have a limited budget, you may need to sacrifice quality to meet the deadline. You might opt for a lower-cost ghostwriter who works faster, but the result might be a book that doesn't fully meet your expectations in terms of voice, depth, or engagement. In this case, while the book is finished on time and within budget, it might not effectively communicate your expertise or connect with readers in the way you'd hoped.

Navigating the Triangle: Finding the Right Balance

Every book project comes with trade-offs, so what are you willing to sacrifice? If you want a book that will truly represent your expertise and brand, you must be prepared to invest time and money into the process. If your timeline is tight, be prepared to adjust your expectations on the level of quality or consider how much you're willing to invest financially.

Ask yourself three honest questions: how much time can you dedicate to this project, how much are you willing to invest financially, and what level of quality do you expect?

Ultimately, choosing two of the three factors, time, quality, and cost, will help you achieve the outcome you desire. It's a delicate balance, but once you understand how these three factors intersect, you can make informed decisions about the book writing process and set realistic goals.

The Elephant in the Room: Why Not Use AI?

Michael thought he had found a shortcut.

He was busy, running a business, managing clients, and barely finding time to breathe. Writing a book? That felt like flying in a spaceship to the moon.

Then he started hearing about AI. ChatGPT. Jasper. Bard. Every headline screamed about how these tools could crank out entire books in minutes. No writer needed. No weeks of struggling to get words on the page. Just type in a prompt and, poof!, let AI do the work.

So, one night, Michael sat at his desk, cracked his knuckles, and thought, *Let's see what this thing can do.*

He typed in a detailed prompt, pressed Generate, and within seconds, AI had spit out an entire chapter. It was fast. It was structured. It even sounded almost professional.

"This is it!" he thought. "This is how I'll finally write my book."

He kept going, feeding the AI more instructions, refining a few sections, and within a couple of days, he had a full draft in hand.

A whole book written in record time. No late nights staring at a blank page. No hiring an expensive ghostwriter.

It felt like magic.

Until he sat down and read it.

The Illusion of Effortless Content

At first glance, the book looked polished.

The chapters were structured.

But then Michael started reading.

And something felt... off.

The words were there. The structure was there. But something was missing.

It didn't sound like him.

It was flat, like an article copied and pasted from a dozen different sources, stitched together without personality or originality.

Michael wanted his book to work for him, to build trust, establish authority, and attract clients.

The insights were surface level. The writing was generic. There was no depth, no emotion, no connection.

Instead? A 200-page corporate snoozefest.

It wasn't forgettable. It was worse than bad. It was replaceable.

And in business, replaceable is worse than bad.

Michael decided to test the waters. He sent the AI-generated manuscript to a few trusted colleagues, people who understood his brand and knew his expertise. He expected a few small edits. What did he get instead?

"This doesn't sound like you at all." "It's technically fine, but there's nothing new here, nothing that makes me want to keep reading." "Honestly? It feels like a blog post stitched together from generic advice I've seen a hundred times before."

Michael's face burned as he stared at the screen, his stomach twisting.

He had been excited about AI's speed, until now. Now, all he felt was embarrassment.

His book was supposed to set him apart. Instead, it made him sound like everyone else.

And then came the sucker punch: If I publish this, people will know I faked it.

The whole point of the book was to build trust. But what happens when people can tell you took a shortcut?

What happens when they see right through it?

He felt sick. He had a book, but it wasn't his book. If he published this, people wouldn't be impressed, they'd be underwhelmed. Worse, they might see right through it. And if they did, what would that do to his credibility?

Michael's stomach twisted. This wasn't dull. It was dangerous. The whole reason he was writing a book was to stand out, to demonstrate his authority. But instead, AI had created something that made him sound replaceable. His expertise had been flattened into bland, forgettable content, one that didn't inspire, didn't persuade, and worst of all, didn't make people want to work with him.

Readers Want More Than Information. They Want Connection

Michael realized something critical: people don't buy books. They buy into the person behind them.

His book wasn't words on a page, it was supposed to be an extension of his brand.

It needed to reflect his voice, share his real-life experiences, and make readers feel like they were sitting across from him learning from someone they trusted. It needed his passion and his heart.

Instead, the AI-generated text was content.

> Content isn't enough.

Because anyone can write about leadership. Or business strategy. Or personal development.

Michael had to see the difference for himself. He took one of the AI-generated passages and compared it to something he had written in the past.

Here's what the AI produced:

It wasn't wrong, but it wasn't right either.

It was the kind of thing you'd skim past in a generic LinkedIn post. Nothing new. Nothing memorable. Nothing that made you stop and think.

Then, Michael rewrote it in his own voice:

The transformation was undeniable.

The AI version had information; his version had real experience. The AI version sounded professional; his version sounded like someone you'd actually want to follow. The AI version could've been written by anyone; his version could've only come from him.

That's when it clicked. AI could generate words, but it couldn't live the experiences behind them. It couldn't tell a real story. It couldn't connect. And if it couldn't do that, what was the point?

What makes a book valuable is the unique insights, real stories, and personal wisdom that only the author can bring to the table.

AI couldn't do that.

And Michael's audience? They would know.

In a world where authenticity is more valuable than ever, readers can sense when something feels off. They don't want information, they want a connection with the author. They want to hear about real struggles, real wins, and real lessons learned.

AI doesn't have life experience. It doesn't struggle, and it doesn't learn.

And that means it can never create a book that truly connects with readers.

The Uncanny Valley of AI Writing

Michael wasn't the only one who had fallen into the AI writing trap.

A few weeks ago, I had a friend who was excited to show me his new book. He had been working on it for months, and I could tell he was proud of it.

But within one second of opening the file, I looked at him and said, "You wrote this with AI."

His jaw dropped. "How did you know?" he asked, stunned.

"I knew it before I even finished the first sentence. AI writing has a distinct feeling, the kind that makes your brain hesitate, even if you can't quite put your finger on why."

It's technically correct. The grammar is clean. The sentences flow logically.

But something is... off.

The words are too perfect, so polished that they lose their personality. The rhythm feels unnatural. The emotions feel forced. It reads like a person who's trying to sound human, rather than someone being human.

And that's when I realized something.

AI writing falls straight into the Uncanny Valley.

The Uncanny Valley is a concept in robotics and animation that describes the unsettling feeling people get when something looks almost human, but not quite.

Think about Disney's 2019 remake of The Lion King.

The CGI was incredible, so realistic that the lions, warthogs, and hyenas looked like actual animals. But something was missing.

The faces moved, but the emotions didn't. The voices spoke, but the soul was missing. It looked real, but it wasn't.

That's because the more something tries to mimic reality, the more unsettling it becomes when it falls short.

It's why people still prefer the 1994 animated version of The Lion King over the hyper-realistic remake. The hand-drawn animation wasn't trying to be real; it embraced the human touch of expressive characters and storytelling.

The same thing happens with AI-generated writing.

It looks real, it sounds real, but the moment you start reading...

Something feels off.

Your brain knows it's missing something. The flow is too robotic. The words feel empty. The passion isn't there.

And when that happens, the reader disconnects.

The Risk of Misinformation and AI Hallucinations

The more Michael read through his AI-generated book, the worse it got.

Not only did it sound robotic, but it also contained several completely false statements.

AI isn't a writing tool; it's a predictive tool. It doesn't know anything. It doesn't verify facts. It doesn't understand context.

It simply guesses what the next word should be based on patterns in data.

And that means AI can create entire paragraphs that sound professional and authoritative, while being completely inaccurate.

As Michael read through his book, he found it had misquoted research, made up sources, and cited statistics that didn't exist.

This is what AI researchers call hallucinations, when AI fabricates information out of thin air but presents it with total confidence.

Michael realized that if he had published this book without fact-checking, his credibility would have been on the line.

Readers trust authors to provide real, reliable insights. One wrong fact, one misleading statement, and that trust disappears.

Michael's book wasn't a marketing tool, it was a credibility test. And one bad fact could cost him more than sales. It could cost him trust.

Trust is everything in business. A single AI-generated mistake wouldn't embarrass him, it could make clients second-guess his entire expertise.

And that was a risk he wasn't willing to take.

The Turning Point: When Michael Got It Right

Michael could have given up at that point.

Instead, he took a different approach.

Instead of using AI to replace the writing process, he partnered with a professional ghostwriter who could craft a book aligned with his business goals, capture his authentic voice, weave in personal stories that made it relatable, show his passion and heart, and fact-check the content so it was credible and valuable.

The difference was night and day.

For the first time, his book felt real. It wasn't "content." It was a strategic business asset, a tool that positioned him as an expert, resonated with readers, and made an impact.

When he handed the finished book to potential clients, their reactions were immediate:

"I feel like you're talking directly to me." "This book made me think differently about my business." "I need to work with you. When can we start?"

That's when Michael knew he had finally created the book he had always wanted.

The Bottom Line: Your Story Deserves More Than Automation

So, should you use AI to write your book?

The truth is, AI is a tool.

AI can help brainstorm ideas, assist with outlining, and speed up parts of the writing process. But it cannot replace strategy, storytelling, or real human connection.

Michael learned this the hard way. AI gave him words, but it didn't give him a message that mattered. It didn't create something that truly represented him.

And at the end of the day, that's what separates a book that gets forgotten from a book that builds a brand.

A book isn't words. It's your voice. Your credibility. Your legacy.

AI can't create that, but you can.

Final Thoughts: The Real Takeaway

Michael learned something that day.

AI could generate text. But it couldn't capture a story.

AI could write about leadership. But it couldn't be a leader.

If he wanted a book that mattered, one that inspired, engaged, and built trust, he had to do it the right way.

With a human voice.

With real stories.

With his perspective.

Because at the end of the day?

People don't follow books. They follow authors.

And an AI can't be an author, only a content machine.

Why You Need a Ghostwriter

James had built a thriving career as a corporate strategist. His insights were in demand, his calendar packed, and his name carried weight in the industry. But every time he pitched a major client or applied for a high-profile speaking gig, the response was the same.

"You have incredible experience," event organizers told him. "But do you have a book?"

James stiffened. He knew exactly what was coming next. The event organizer's voice was polite, but the question hit like a hammer: *Do you have a book*?"

He had tried to start writing, but between client calls, meetings, and travel, the manuscript never made it past a few rough paragraphs. Every attempt ended in frustration, and the book remained an unfinished dream.

Frustrated, James finally made a bold decision, he hired a ghostwriter. Instead of spending months staring at a blinking cursor, he spent a few focused sessions talking through his ideas, clarifying his message, and refining his expertise.

The ghostwriter took care of the rest, crafting structure, shaping the story, and ensuring the book still sounded like him.

Six months later, James held the finished book in his hands. A book that positioned him as an industry authority. A book that changed his career.

What happened next?

He started landing major speaking engagements without chasing them. His speaking fees tripled because his credibility was undeniable. And a major business magazine featured him — his book had made him the go-to expert in his field.

James realized something that changed the trajectory of his career: the best experts aren't always the ones getting noticed. The ones with books are.

James isn't alone. Some people never get far enough to discover that the real problem is the process, not the ideas. Maya, a successful entrepreneur, was convinced she just needed time.

Every weekend, she blocked out hours to write. At first, she felt unstoppable. Words poured onto the page. She imagined the book launch, the press, the opportunities.

Then, the cracks started to show.

She rewrote the introduction, again.

Her ideas felt scattered.

Her chapters lacked structure.

The excitement faded. Doubt crept in.

Six months later, her progress? Five unfinished chapters. And worse, she had stopped writing entirely. The book that was supposed to elevate her brand was now an unfinished project collecting dust.

Finally, frustrated, she reached out to a ghostwriter. Within two months, they had more progress than she'd made in an entire year. Instead of agonizing over drafts, she talked through her ideas, and her ghostwriter transformed them into a polished manuscript.

Looking back, Maya had one regret: she should have hired a ghostwriter sooner.

Because trying to "figure it out" alone? It had cost her more than time, it had cost her momentum, confidence, and real business opportunities.

What a Ghostwriter Actually Does for You

Hiring a ghostwriter isn't about cutting corners, it's about being smart with your time. You could spend months wrestling with words, or you could focus on what you do best while your ghostwriter brings your ideas to life.

More importantly, a skilled ghostwriter captures your voice. One of the biggest fears people have about hiring a ghostwriter is that their book won't sound like them. A professional knows how to listen, adapt, and refine your words so that the final product reflects you, only more polished, more refined, and more impactful.

The result? A high-quality, professionally written book that elevates your brand, establishes your authority, and opens new doors, without sacrificing your time, energy, or sanity.

Will a Ghostwriter Make It Sound Like Me?

This is the most common concern people have about hiring a ghostwriter.

The questions that stop most people sound like this: "Will it sound like me?" "Will I still have control over the book?" "Will it reflect my ideas?"

Here's the reality:

A ghostwriter's job isn't to rewrite you, it's to bring out your voice, refined and polished.

They study how you speak. They listen to your phrasing, tone, and storytelling style. They make sure that when people read your book, they hear you in every sentence.

It's like having a professional songwriter craft lyrics for a musician. The musician still delivers the performance, the passion, the message. The songwriter helps shape it into something powerful.

What makes this even better?

You stay in control.

You approve every chapter. You set the vision. You decide what gets included and what doesn't.

> A ghostwriter is a partner, not a replacement. They help you do what you wouldn't have time to do alone.

The difference between staying stuck and getting your book written isn't talent, luck, or years of experience. It comes down to one decision: act and get help, or keep waiting, convincing yourself that "someday" will magically arrive.

The longer you wait, the more ground you hand to people with less experience, fewer credentials, and half your expertise. They're not better than you. They just showed up with a book.

Your expertise deserves a platform, and your ideas deserve an audience. Your book deserves to exist.

All you have to do is take the first step.

The Barriers to Writing a Book

You Want to Write a Book. So Why Hasn't It Happened Yet?

Miguel had spent years perfecting his craft. His business was steady, his clients happy. But lately, he couldn't shake the feeling that he was falling behind. How were others, some with half his experience, getting the spotlight?

They weren't better at their jobs, but they had something Miguel didn't: a book to prove it.

For years, Miguel had told himself he would write one too. He had the expertise. He had the stories. He had insights that could change lives. But every time he sat down to start, something stopped him.

At first, he blamed timing. Work never seemed to slow down, and he kept pushing his book to the side.

Then, when he finally tried to write, he realized his knowledge didn't translate to the page as easily as he thought. He'd type a few sentences, then delete them. The book in his head was clear but getting it onto paper felt impossible.

And when he tried to organize everything into something readable, the sheer size of the task overwhelmed him.

Like many professionals, he shelved the idea, telling himself he'd revisit it later.

Until the day he saw his former colleague in a business magazine, holding up their book, with the headline:

"Industry Leader Publishes Groundbreaking New Book."

Miguel skimmed the article, his stomach tightening. His old colleague wasn't more experienced, but now, he was the name people turned to. All because he had a book.

So why hadn't he written his yet?

Because, like most people, he ran into three barriers that stop almost everyone.

Barrier #1: No Time

Miguel was always busy, moving from client calls to meetings, strategy sessions, and proposals. Whenever he set aside time for the book, a new fire needed putting out. The urgent always won.

At first, he thought he needed a slow season. He told himself, *"I'll start when work calms down."* But work never calmed down.

There was always another project, another deadline, another client who needed him. Days turned into months. Months turned into years.

And yet, in the back of his mind, the book was always there. Waiting.

But waiting wasn't helping.

While Miguel waited for the perfect moment, others published and passed him by.

Barrier #2: Writing Is Harder Than It Looks

Miguel had assumed that because he was an expert, writing his book would be simple.

It wasn't.

The first time he sat down to write, he expected the words to flow. Instead, he stared at the screen, unsure where to begin.

When he finally did write, he second-guessed everything. Did it sound professional? Was it clear? Did it ramble too much? He'd reread sentences over and over, tweaking and adjusting, but something always felt off.

The frustration grew. He knew he had valuable insights, but every attempt to put them into words felt clunky and uninspired. He wanted the book to be great, not done. But the gap between what he knew and how to express it felt impossible to bridge.

The more he struggled, the more he questioned whether he could do it at all.

Barrier #3: Overwhelm

Even when he managed to get a few ideas onto paper, Miguel quickly realized he had too much to say.

Some days, he thought his book should focus on leadership. Other days, he was convinced it should be about business growth. Then, he'd remember client success stories that deserved a place, and suddenly, his book felt like five different books smashed together.

Each time he tried to sort through his ideas, his confidence took a hit.

Should he start with an outline? Should he start writing and figure it out later?

The uncertainty was exhausting. And instead of making progress, he let it sit.

Another month went by. Then another.

And the book, the one that could position him as an industry leader, remained unfinished.

The Turning Point: How a Ghostwriter Changed Everything

Instead of forcing himself to struggle through the writing process alone, he hired a ghostwriter.

Speaking opportunities opened up. His book got him featured in industry publications. High-value clients reached out to him, not the other way around.

For the first time, his expertise wasn't something people knew about, it was something they could see.

Your book isn't words on a page. It's your credibility. Your authority. Your opportunity to reach people in a way nothing else can.

In the next chapter, we explore the different paths to getting your book written — from doing it yourself to working with a ghostwriter — so you can choose the one that fits your goals, your timeline, and your life.

Finding the Right Path for Your Book

So, you know you need a book. You've read about why waiting is costing you opportunities, and you're ready to get started. The next question is: How do you get it written?

You have more options than you might think. Some will save you money, but it costs you time. Others will get the job done but sacrifice quality. And then there are the options that ensure your book is done right, the ones that protect your reputation, enhance your brand, and give you something you can be proud of.

Let's break them down.

Option 1: Writing It Yourself

Meet Jake.

Jake is a corporate consultant with years of experience and a wealth of knowledge. Clients constantly tell him, "You should write a book." So, one day, he decides to do it himself.

He downloaded a fancy writing app, created a detailed outline, and set an ambitious goal. The first week was exciting, and he got a few pages down. By the second week, he started missing sessions. By the third month, the manuscript sat untouched, buried under client projects.

His writing sessions grew fewer and farther between. Client work takes priority. Life gets in the way. His manuscript sat half-finished in a folder on his laptop, gathering digital dust.

Jake wanted to write his book. He had the expertise. But without structure, deadlines, and accountability, his book never got finished.

Pros:

Writing it yourself gives you full control over every word, sentence, and story, along with the personal satisfaction of knowing you wrote it yourself, and technically no financial cost — if you don't count the time.

Cons:

But it's time-consuming in ways most professionals underestimate — writing a book takes hundreds of hours, and most people can't afford to put their business or life on hold that long. Knowing your subject doesn't mean you know how to structure a book or keep readers hooked. And the majority of first-time authors never finish; they get stuck, overwhelmed, or lose momentum.

If you have time, patience, and a natural ability to write, this path can work. But if you're already stretched thin or unsure where to start, it's a slow and frustrating process.

Option 2: AI Writing (Been There, Done That)

Remember Michael from earlier in this book?

Michael thought AI was the shortcut he needed. He generated chapters in minutes, compiled them, and felt like he had cracked the system.

Until he read the book.

It was generic, it didn't sound like him, and it lacked depth, emotion, and originality.

His trusted colleagues told him it wasn't good enough. If he published it, his credibility would take a hit.

Michael realized the truth about AI: It's a tool, not a replacement for real expertise, experience, and storytelling.

AI doesn't sound like you, fills your book with generic forgettable content, and can contain false information that damages your credibility.

AI is a tool, not a solution. If you want a book that builds authority and trust, AI alone won't cut it.

Option 3: Cheap Ghostwriters & Content Mills

If you start searching for ghostwriters online, you'll find people offering to write an entire book for $500, $1,000, maybe even $2,000. At first, this sounds like a bargain, after all, writing a book is hard work, and if someone's willing to do it cheaply, why not?

Here's why not.

These writers aren't investing weeks of effort, deep research, or careful craftsmanship. They're pumping out cookie-cutter content, often outsourced, and sometimes even plagiarized.

Meet Karen.

Karen is a marketing consultant who understands the power of a book. She finds a ghostwriter online offering to write a full book for $1,500.

"This is perfect," she thinks.

The ghostwriter promises a 30-day turnaround. Everything seems smooth, until she gets the first draft.

The writing was stiff, it sounded nothing like her, and the content was generic and repetitive.

A plagiarism check revealed entire paragraphs lifted from blog posts, word for word.

Karen faced an uncomfortable choice: publish a mediocre, copy-paste book that might hurt her brand, or start over and waste both time and money.

Karen decided to publish anyway, hoping no one would notice. Within days, a client emailed her: "This book doesn't sound like you." The damage was done.

Pros:

The appeal is low cost — if budget is your top priority, this is the cheapest way to get a book written — and many of these writers promise quick turnaround, sometimes thirty days or less.

Cons:

The downsides are significant: these books are often generic, repetitive, and uninspired, and won't impress anyone. Many cheap ghostwriters reuse material or copy from other sources. And if your name is on the cover, your reputation is on the line — a bad book can do more harm than no book at all.

Option 4: Premium Ghostwriters (That's Me)

If you want a high-quality book that sounds like you, enhances your brand, and positions you as a go-to expert with something valuable to say, you need a professional.

A premium ghostwriter doesn't crank out words, they partner with you to craft a book that reflects your expertise, your voice, and your goals. They take the time to understand your story, organize your ideas, and create something compelling, strategic, and marketable.

> For professionals who see their book as a business asset, one that brings credibility, leads, and speaking opportunities, a premium ghostwriter is the best choice.

Ted is a leadership speaker who knows his book needs to match the quality of his brand. He can't afford a book that sounds amateurish.

Instead of trying to do it himself or hiring a cheap freelancer, he hires a premium ghostwriter.

He needed a ghostwriter who could capture his voice so every sentence sounded like something he'd actually say, structure the book strategically so it flowed and delivered value, and save him time so he could stay focused on his business while the book got written.

Months later, Ted holds his book in his hands. It's polished, professional, and exactly what he envisioned.

Phil, the co-founder of Nike and author of Shoe Dog, built Nike from a scrappy startup into a global empire, but when it came time to write his memoir, he knew he needed help. He wasn't a writer; he was a businessman. And if his story was going to do justice to his journey, it needed to be more than a collection of facts. It had to capture the grit, struggles, and victories that defined his career.

So, he hired J.R. Moehringer, a premium ghostwriter and Pulitzer Prize-winning journalist, to bring his story to life.

Moehringer didn't write a book for Phil. He immersed himself in Phil's world, interviewed him extensively, and captured his voice, personality, and vision. The result? Shoe Dog became one of the best business memoirs ever written, praised for its raw, engaging storytelling and emotional depth, something a DIY book or an AI-generated manuscript could never achieve.

Pros:

A skilled ghostwriter studies your tone, phrasing, and personality so the book sounds like you. The process is time-efficient — you get a finished book without spending months struggling through drafts. The structure and storytelling are professional, polished, and strategically designed to achieve your goals. And everything is written from scratch — no AI, no fluff, no recycled content.

Cons:

The tradeoffs are real: a premium ghostwriter is a significant investment, often ranging from $15,000 to $75,000 or more depending on length and complexity, and quality books take time — expect three to six months, not thirty days.

Who is this option for?

If your book is meant to enhance your authority, grow your business, or land speaking engagements, this is the smartest option. A high-quality book opens doors and pays for itself in opportunities.

Option 5: Celebrity & High-End Ghostwriters

Meet Philip. He was a major player in the corporate world, but his legacy wasn't solidified. He wanted a book that would cement his place as an authority, something that would be read, quoted, and taken seriously at the highest levels.

He knew that slapping together a basic book wasn't going to cut it. If he wanted to be in the same league as the biggest names in business, he needed a top-tier ghostwriter, someone with experience, connections, and storytelling chops to craft a book that could stand alongside the best.

That's what high-end ghostwriters do.

Take The Art of the Deal. Donald Trump's name is on the cover, but Tony Schwartz was the true architect of the book. It wasn't a collection of business advice; it was a brand-building masterpiece. Schwartz took Trump's ideas, stories, and persona and wove them into a compelling narrative that shaped his public image for decades.

Schwartz didn't write the book; he shaped a persona that Trump would leverage for decades. This was more than ghostwriting — it was personal brand engineering on a global scale.

Another example? The Other Guy Blinked: How Pepsi Won the Cola Wars, ghostwritten by J. Patrick Wright for Pepsi's CEO, Roger Enrico. This book wasn't corporate storytelling, it was a strategic move in a billion-dollar battle. The book solidified Enrico as a bold, aggressive leader, framing Pepsi as the underdog-turned-victor in a fight against Coke.

High-end ghostwriters do more than write books, they help you tell your story in a way that shapes how the world sees you. They are storytellers, strategists, and brand architects rolled into one.

Pros:

Celebrity and high-end ghostwriters deliver top-tier quality — highly polished, thoroughly researched, designed for major impact. The process is largely hands-off, with the ghostwriter sometimes managing the publishing process as well. Many also bring industry connections to top publishers, PR teams, and speaking agencies.

Cons:

Unless you're a high-profile figure with major backing or a huge platform, this level is overkill — and some of these projects take a year or more to complete.

Who is this option for?

If you're a celebrity, politician, or Fortune 500 CEO, this is your lane. But for most professionals and business owners, a premium ghostwriter (Option 4) is the better balance of quality, cost, and impact.

Which Option is Right for You?

Ultimately, the right path depends on what you need. Here's a quick way to decide:

If you love writing and have the time, write it yourself. If you want something fast and cheap, content mills will get you a book, but not a good one. If you need high quality but don't have a celebrity budget, premium ghostwriting is your best bet. And if you're famous and need a book positioned for the bestseller lists, you'll want celebrity-level help.

The biggest mistake people make? Choosing an option that doesn't align with their goals.

If your book is meant to grow your business, attract clients, or establish you as an authority, quality matters. And that means choosing the right ghostwriter, one who understands your voice, your brand, and your audience.

So, which path will you take?

In the next chapter, we'll break down exactly how the ghostwriting process works, so you know what to expect when you decide to get your book written.

Book Coaching

Not everyone wants to hand their book off to someone else. For many first-time authors, writing their own story is non-negotiable. The process might be messy, time-consuming, or even overwhelming, but they want their words on the page. They don't want to do it alone.

That's where a good coach makes all the difference.

Book coaching is the in-between path, not quite DIY, and not fully outsourced. It gives you the guidance you need without giving up the writing itself. It's a collaborative process where you write the book yourself, but with structure, accountability, and expert feedback guiding you every step of the way. Your coach doesn't take over the keyboard, they help you find the confidence to sit at it consistently.

You're the one writing it. Your coach is the steady hand that helps you keep going when it gets hard.

A Different Kind of Writing Support

Unlike ghostwriting, where someone else turns your ideas into polished prose, book coaching leaves the creative control firmly in your hands. A coach isn't there to write your book for you. They're there to help you write it well and finish it.

Coaches help untangle cluttered ideas, offer professional-level feedback without judgment, and make sure your book isn't getting written, it's getting written with clarity, focus, and purpose. And perhaps most importantly, they keep you from quitting when life gets busy or imposter syndrome creeps in.

Rather than handing your voice off, you're developing it, with guidance from someone who's helped others do the same.

Who Book Coaching Is For (And Who It's Not)

Book coaching isn't for everyone, and that's the point.

It's ideal for authors who want to write their own book but need help navigating the process. It's for people who have a message but not a map. It's especially helpful for professionals writing their first business book, thought leaders refining their story, or memoirists processing a personal experience through the written word.

If you want the book to reflect who you are, not your name on the cover, but your tone in every paragraph, coaching helps you get there.

But if you're short on time, not interested in learning the writing process, or you want to hand off the task to someone else and move on with your business, ghostwriting may be a better fit. The key is knowing what kind of author you want to be, and what kind of experience you want to have along the way.

Real Authors, Real Coaching Results

Sophia lost her husband and turned to journaling as a way to heal. When she realized her story could help others, she tried to turn it into a book. But grief is messy, and so was the writing. Her book coach helped her shape the raw, emotional material into a powerful, readable memoir, one that still felt honest, but was structured to serve her readers too.

Tom had been running productivity workshops for years and knew he had a unique framework. He didn't have time to learn how to be a professional writer, but he didn't want someone else writing it for him either. With a coach, he broke down the book chapter by chapter, built a writing rhythm, and turned his framework into something tangible and polished, without losing his voice.

Carmen, a therapist, knew her material inside out, but struggled with clarity and flow. Her writing was more clinical than conversational. Her coach helped her soften the tone, sharpen the message, and create a book that clients and peers now recommend. The experience didn't produce a book, it made her a better communicator.

How Book Coaching Actually Works

The coaching relationship is built on consistent, collaborative interaction. You meet with your coach to develop your book's outline, set realistic writing goals, and build a timeline. From there, you write, and your coach reviews your drafts, offering notes on clarity, flow, voice, and structure.

Some authors work with a coach weekly; others check in twice a month. Some send full chapters; others submit in smaller bursts. The process flexes around your needs, but it never leaves you guessing what to do next.

Coaching relationships often last three to six months, though some books take longer depending on depth and complexity. And at the end, you walk away with more than a manuscript. You walk away with the skills and confidence to do it again.

Ghostwriting or Book Coaching? Which Path Is Right for You?

You don't have to choose sides. Both paths can lead to a strong, professional book. The difference lies in how you want to get there, and what you want the process to feel like.

Choose ghostwriting if:

Ghostwriting is the right path if you're short on time and need a book done, if writing isn't your strength or interest, if you want to be the expert rather than the writer, or if you care more about the finished product than the process of creating it.

Choose book coaching if:

Book coaching is the right path if you want to write your book yourself but don't know how to start, if you want to grow as a writer and find your voice, if your story is personal and the words need to come from you, if you've started but keep getting stuck, or if you need deadlines, structure, and a professional who won't let you quit.

Whichever way you go, choose the path that fits your goals, and how involved you want to be in the process.

The Guide – How Ghostwriters Make You the Star

You already have the knowledge, the stories, and the insights. But turning that into a book? That's where most people get stuck. A ghostwriter helps you take what's in your head and shape it into something powerful, readable, and uniquely yours.

You don't have to put your business on hold to write a book. That's the advantage of working with a ghostwriter. You talk. You share your best ideas. You bring the raw material, your stories, your insights, the things that matter. While you stay focused on your work, your ghostwriter turns it into a book that's authentically you.

When the Book Feels Impossible

Danielle stared at the calendar. The first ghostwriting interview was in an hour, and her stomach tightened. She wondered, do I even have anything worth saying? What if my stories are too technical? What if I go through all this effort and it doesn't work?

Danielle had made the commitment. This book was happening. She had hired a ghostwriter, set up the first interview, and cleared her schedule for the process.

But as the call approached, nerves crept in.

She had spent her career in cybersecurity, working her way up from analyst to executive. She had been in the trenches, handling massive data breaches, developing security strategies for global corporations, and testifying about cyber threats before government panels.

She knew this industry inside and out. But writing a book about it? That was a different challenge.

What if her stories were too technical? What if people outside cybersecurity wouldn't understand them? What if her book didn't have a clear theme?

The morning of the interview, she skimmed through her notes; stories of attacks prevented, companies saved, and the constant battle to stay ahead of cybercriminals. She had knowledge that could help business leaders, security teams, and even everyday people protect themselves in an increasingly digital world.

But how did she turn that into a compelling book?

When the call started, her ghostwriter asked a simple question:

"If you could get one message across in this book, what would it be?"

Danielle hesitated for a moment, then spoke.

"Most businesses think cybersecurity is an IT problem. It's not. It's a leadership problem. And if leaders don't get ahead of it, they're going to find themselves cleaning up a mess they never saw coming."

As soon as she said it, something clicked.

The ghostwriter nodded. "That's it. That's your book."

She exhaled. She didn't need to have it all figured out. She needed to start.

What a Ghostwriter Really Does

Danielle's concern was common. A lot of professionals hesitate before working with a ghostwriter because they think they need everything figured out in advance. They believe they need a fully developed outline, a structured argument, or even a draft before getting started.

That's not reality.

A ghostwriter doesn't expect you to come in with a perfectly formed book idea. They help you find it.

Danielle didn't need to have every chapter mapped out. She needed to show up and share what she knew best, and the ghostwriter would take care of the structure, the organization, and making sure it all made sense to the reader.

Ghostwriters don't write. They listen.

They pull the best stories from you; the insights you might not even realize are valuable. They help you get to the heart of what you want to say, and make sure it lands with the people who need it most. They shape your knowledge into a compelling narrative that keeps people engaged, even if the subject is complex or technical.

In Danielle's case, the ghostwriter helped her frame the book not as a cybersecurity manual, but as a wake-up call for business leaders who were unknowingly putting their companies at risk.

The book wasn't going to be about threats and data breaches, it was going to be about leadership, accountability, and the future of business security.

That shift changed everything.

How a Ghostwriter Captures Your Voice

Danielle needed a book that reflected her experience, authority, and personality, one that felt authentic.

A few weeks into the process, Danielle received an early draft of the introduction. She opened the document, took a deep breath, and started reading. Halfway through the page, she stopped. She knew these were her words, but something about them felt... sharper. More polished. It sounded like her, clearer, stronger, more impactful.

That's when she realized, it still sounded like her. Just sharper. Stronger. More impactful.

> A great ghostwriter does more than write. They study how you speak.

From the first interview, they listen to your tone, your phrasing, and your storytelling style. If you have existing content, blog posts, speeches, interviews, they use that to capture your natural voice.

Throughout the process, they draft sample sections and get your feedback. If something doesn't feel right, they adjust it until it does.

By the time the book is done, it doesn't sound like you, it is you, with a level of polish and structure that makes it compelling for a wider audience.

Danielle didn't have to worry about whether the book would feel like hers.

She was still the expert. She was still the voice behind every idea.

The ghostwriter helped bring it to life.

Real Success Stories: How Ghostwriting Changes Everything

For cybersecurity professionals like Danielle, writing a book isn't about sharing knowledge, it's about credibility, visibility, and influence.

Take Monica, a cybersecurity consultant who had spent years advising Fortune 500 companies. She had the knowledge, but no time to write a book.

Before her book, Monica was competing with dozens of other cybersecurity consultants. After her book? She stopped competing. The phone calls changed.

"I read your book and knew you were the expert we needed."

Now, instead of chasing clients, they came to her.

Her book positioned her as a sought-after expert. She started getting keynote speaking requests from industry conferences and invitations to join high-level advisory boards.

Then there was Sharon, a CISO who wanted to warn executives about the hidden risks in their security strategies. Her book was picked up by business publications, and soon, she was featured in major media outlets discussing real-world cyber threats. Companies that had never considered her before started reaching out, ready to pay top dollar for her expertise.

And Owen, a retired intelligence analyst, wanted to turn his decades of cybersecurity experience into a book that would educate the next generation. His book became a must-read in security training programs, and within months, he was invited to teach workshops and consult for government agencies.

Each of them had the expertise.

The only difference between them and others in their industry?

They had a book.

Real Results from Real Books

A client of mine — a business consultant who'd spent twenty years building expertise nobody outside his firm knew about — sent me a message three months after his book launched. A Fortune 500 company had reached out, not because of a cold pitch or a LinkedIn post, but because their VP had read the book on a flight and forwarded it to the executive team. He got the engagement. It was the largest of his career.

Your Book Isn't Just Paper. It's a Platform

John figured his book would help a little, maybe make networking easier. A few free copies at conferences, a credibility boost on his website. But a week after launch, his inbox told a different story.

And then came the real shift. Clients who used to hesitate started reaching out, ready to work with him before he even pitched them. A high-profile conference organizer asked him to lead a panel. A major business publication featured his insights.

One book, one decision to finally share what he knew, changed everything.

The Tangible Benefits of Publishing a Book

A book isn't a product, it's leverage. It's the difference between chasing opportunities and having them come to you.

When event organizers look for speakers, they go for those with books. When media outlets need expert opinions, they reach out to published authors. And when high-value clients want to work with the best, they trust the people who wrote the book on the subject.

It happens again and again. One consultant published his book and raised his rates by 50%, clients didn't blink. A speaker who used to get ignored started booking keynotes. And a professional who'd spent years being overlooked? Her book put her on the map.

Once their book was out, authors started hearing things they hadn't expected: invitations to be podcast guests, requests to speak at events, and messages from clients who'd read the book and were already sold before getting on a call.

That's how real credibility is earned, not by waiting to be discovered, but by publishing something that proves you belong.

A book makes your ideas tangible. It turns your knowledge into something people can hold, reference, and recommend. Unlike a blog post or a social media update, a book has staying power. It doesn't disappear in a feed, and it doesn't get buried in an inbox. It sits on bookshelves, in offices, on nightstands.

And the more people read it, the more your influence grows.

The Intangible Rewards of Writing a Book

The benefits of a book aren't external. Something shifts inside you when you become an author.

Before the book, your expertise feels scattered, like pieces of a puzzle you haven't quite put together. But when you sit down to write, those pieces lock into place. You gain total clarity on your message. You sharpen your ideas, refine your knowledge, and walk away knowing exactly what you stand for.

Then there's the sense of accomplishment. Everyone says they want to write a book. Few do. Holding your book in your hands, knowing that you took your knowledge, your experience, and your ideas and turned them into something real. It's a feeling unlike anything else.

And it lasts. A book isn't a blog post that gets buried in a feed. It isn't a speech that fades as soon as the event is over. A book outlives you. Your words, your insights, your story, they keep working long after you've written them. Years from now, someone will pick up your book, read your words, and be changed by them.

That's the power of a book.

And beyond the personal transformation, a book forces you to level up. When you write a book, you can no longer hide behind imposter syndrome. You can no longer second-guess your authority. A book requires you to step fully into your expertise, and once you do, there's no going back.

The Cost of Doing Nothing

But what happens if you don't publish it?

Or maybe you'll still be telling yourself, "I should start that book."

Maybe you'll see someone else land the speaking gig you wanted, write the book you had in mind, or get the media coverage you always dreamed of. And you'll know that the only difference between them and you is that they took action, and you didn't.

That's the real cost of waiting.

Overcoming Your Hesitations

At some point in almost every conversation I have with a prospective client, there's a pause. Not a long one. Just a beat. And then they say some version of the same thing: "I know I need to do this. But..." The hesitation has many names — time, money, self-doubt, perfectionism — but underneath it, they all mean the same thing: fear that the book won't be good enough, or that they aren't.

Your Book Is Possible. Even If You Have Doubts

Chris excelled in his field; clients trusted him, colleagues frequently sought his counsel, and he had built a solid reputation.

Yet, every time someone told him, "You should write a book," he nodded, smiled, and changed the subject.

He had plenty of reasons to wait. His schedule was packed. He wasn't sure where to start. And honestly? He wasn't convinced a book would change much.

Then, one day, someone else in his industry published a book.

A competitor with half his experience, weaker results, and fewer credentials.

And suddenly, that person was everywhere. Featured in industry magazines. Speaking at high-profile conferences. Getting the calls Chris used to get.

Chris was no longer the first call for expert advice. Not because he wasn't qualified. Not because his competitor was better.

But that competitor had a book and he didn't. That single difference shifted everything.

That's when it hit him. He wasn't protecting his time, he was losing ground.

Does this resonate with you? You're aware that authoring a book could unlock new opportunities, enhance your authority, and establish your legacy.

So why haven't you started?

For most people, the hesitation isn't about writing, it's about the unknowns.

The doubts sound familiar: what if I don't know how to begin, what if I start and never finish, what if my ideas aren't good enough, what if it's too expensive?

I Don't Know Where to Start

Most first-time authors picture themselves staring at a blank page, struggling to figure out where to begin.

That's not how it works.

A skilled ghostwriter will ask the right questions to pull out the most valuable insights from your experience. They help you uncover the core message of your book, not by making you "come up with it" but by recognizing the value in what you already know.

It's not about forcing yourself into writer mode. It's about showing up as yourself, sharing what you're passionate about, and letting an expert shape it into something powerful.

You don't need to start with a perfect book idea. You need to start talking.

What If I Get Overwhelmed?

A book might seem massive, but here's the truth: you're not writing a book all at once, you're telling your story piece by piece.

Consider constructing a house: you wouldn't attempt to build it in a single day. Initially, you lay the foundation, followed by framing the walls, and later, refining and polishing the details.

That's exactly how ghostwriting works.

We start with a plan — before a single word is written, we map out a clear direction for your book. Then we record: short, structured conversations replace hours of struggling alone at a keyboard. Finally, we shape the book together — instead of overwhelming you with drafts, we move chapter by chapter so the process always feels manageable.

This means you're never drowning in an impossible workload. You're simply collaborating, one step at a time.

What If My Ideas Aren't Strong Enough?

Most authors worry about whether their book will matter.

The fears keep coming: what if it's not original enough, what if no one reads it, what if I put it out there and no one connects with it?

Let's set the record straight.

The goal of your book isn't to present entirely new ideas but to convey them through your unique perspective.

Your experiences, your stories, your insights, they're uniquely yours.

Every great book goes beyond sharing information, it offers a fresh perspective. It gives readers a new way to see, think, or act.

That's why your voice matters.

Because someone out there needs to hear this message from you.

What If It's Not Original Enough?

You've read books on your topic before. You've seen experts talk about the same things you want to cover. So, you wonder: do I have something new to say?

Here's the truth: originality isn't about coming up with something no one has ever heard before. It's about presenting your insights, experiences, and perspective in a way that only you can.

Every successful book stands out not because of a brand-new concept, but because of the voice behind it. There are thousands of leadership books, but people still read *Dare to Lead* by Brené Brown because they connect with her way of explaining things. There are countless business books, but *The 4-Hour Workweek* hit differently because of how Tim Ferriss packaged the message.

Your book isn't about the information, it's about you and the way you deliver it. That's what makes it unique.

What If No One Reads It?

Every author has this fear. You put in the work, you publish your book... and then what? What if it sits there?

But here's what most first-time authors don't realize: books don't have to be bestsellers to be highly valuable.

Your book isn't about selling millions of copies, it's about reaching the right people. If your book brings you three new high-value clients, was it worth it? If it gets you on a major podcast or lands you a speaking gig that changes your career, did it do its job?

Even if only one person reads your book and it changes their life, wasn't it worth writing?

The truth is, most people don't market their books effectively, but if you're strategic, your book will find its audience. And we'll cover exactly how to make that happen later in this book.

What If No One Cares?

You don't want to write a book for the sake of it. You want it to matter. You want it to change the way people think, work, or live.

But impact isn't about how many books you sell; it's about how deeply your message resonates.

Your book might not go viral overnight, but it can still make a significant impact over time. Some of the most influential books in history started as slow burns, spreading through word of mouth and changing industries over time.

And here's the thing: if your book helps even one person make a better decision, avoid a mistake, or gain clarity on something important, it made an impact. And that impact will multiply as your book reaches more people over time.

What If People Criticize It?

The moment you put something out into the world, whether it's a book, a blog, or a business, you open yourself up to opinions.

And yes, some of those opinions will be negative.

But let's put this into perspective: No book has ever been universally liked. Not one. Even the most celebrated books of all time have critics. If Shakespeare and Stephen King have one-star reviews, so will you.

The real question isn't whether you'll face criticism, it's whether you'll let the fear of it hold you back?

Because on the other side of a few naysayers, there will be people who love what you wrote, who needed your insights, and who will be grateful you took the leap.

Don't let a hypothetical hater silence your voice before you even start.

What if I Don't Know How to Market It?

Writing a book is one thing, getting it into people's hands is another. If you're worried about marketing, you're not alone.

Most authors aren't marketers. But that doesn't mean your book won't succeed.

Here's the secret: you don't have to do it alone. There are proven strategies, tools, and experts who can help you spread the word. And you don't need a huge platform to make your book work for you.

Later in this book, we'll cover simple, effective ways to get your book in front of the right audience, without feeling like a pushy salesperson.

For now, know this: if you write the right book, a book that truly delivers value, marketing becomes easier because people will naturally want to share it.

What if writing a book isn't worth the effort?

This is the final hesitation, the one that sneaks in when you're weighing the time, energy, and investment of writing a book.

Let's flip the question around: What's the cost of NOT writing it?

If you don't publish your book:

Without a book, the cost of waiting compounds quietly. You stay in the same place while others step into the spotlight. Competitors claim authority you know should be yours. And you keep repeating the same stories and insights to clients, one conversation at a time, instead of having a book do it for you at scale.

And most importantly, five years from now, will you be happy you waited? Or will you wish you had started?

What If It's Too Expensive?

Writing a book isn't free, and that's a valid concern. But here's the real question: Is it an expense, or is it an investment in your future?

A book isn't another business expense, it's a strategic asset. It works for you long after it's written, building credibility, opening doors, and attracting high-value clients who see you as the go-to authority.

The Cost of Waiting

Maybe you still think now isn't the right time.

But ask yourself this: If not now, when?

The question isn't whether you have what it takes. You do. The question is whether you'll act before someone else does.

The difference? Whether you take action today.

The window doesn't stay open. Someone else in your field is finishing their book right now — and when it lands, they'll have a credibility advantage that's almost impossible to overcome without one of your own.

What Happens Next?

Now that we've tackled the fears that hold most authors back, you're probably wondering, how does ghostwriting work?

How do we go from an idea in your head to a finished book in your hands?

The good news? It's simpler than you think.

A great ghostwriting process is structured, collaborative, and efficient, so you stay involved without feeling overwhelmed.

In the next chapter, we'll break it down step by step:

How we start with your vision and goals, How we build a clear roadmap for your book, How drafts take shape and evolve through collaboration, and How we refine, polish, and get your book publication-ready

By the time we're done, you'll know exactly what to expect, and you'll see how easy it is to finally make your book a reality.

Ghostwriting as an Investment in Your Brand

Think about the last time you hired a professional for something that mattered — a lawyer, an architect, a financial advisor. You didn't pay for their time. You paid for the certainty that it would be done right. A ghostwriter is no different. When you invest in one, you're not paying for words on a page. You're paying for a finished book that works — one that sounds like you, positions you correctly, and keeps generating value long after the check clears.

In the next chapter, we'll dive into why ghostwriting isn't an expense, it's one of the smartest investments you can make. You'll see how professionals have leveraged their books to transform their careers, and why having a ghostwriter ensures you don't just finish a book but that you publish one that makes an impact.

Let's explore how your book can work for you.

When you decide to publish a book, you're not creating a piece of writing, you're making a powerful investment in your brand. A professionally written book can amplify your reputation, establish you as an authority in your field, and open doors to new opportunities that can last for years.

In this chapter, we'll explore how ghostwriting isn't a service, but a long-term strategy that enhances your personal or business brand. We'll look at the ways your book can serve as a tool for growing your influence, gaining credibility, and positioning yourself for success. By understanding the full value of ghostwriting, you'll see that it's an investment that pays dividends long after the book is published.

Your Book Is More Than a Book. It's a Business Asset

When Daniel stepped down as the Chief Operating Officer of a Fortune 500 company, he wasn't planning to retire.

For years, he had led high-performing teams, navigated corporate crises, and built a reputation as a strategic leader. Now, he wanted to take that experience and start his own coaching business, helping executives, founders, and professionals reach the next level in their careers.

There was one problem: no one knew him outside of his corporate circles.

Inside the company, he was a respected leader. Outside? He was another former executive trying to break into the competitive coaching world.

Daniel knew he needed credibility, something that would position him as a sought-after coach, not another business professional offering advice.

That's when he decided to write a book.

At first, he thought about doing it himself. After all, he had written countless reports, whitepapers, and strategic plans. But writing a book was a different beast. He didn't have time to wrestle with structure, storytelling, and the nuances of publishing.

So, he hired a ghostwriter.

Six months later, his book was finished. Three months after that, he was using it to attract high-level coaching clients. Within a year, he was booking paid speaking gigs and growing his brand.

Instead of cold pitching himself as a coach, he sent copies of his book to decision-makers, executives, and business owners.

Some read it and reached out immediately. Some saw it on social media and invited him to speak. Some simply knew his name now, and when they needed an executive coach, they thought of him first.

His book wasn't something to sell. It was his entry point into a new industry.

It positioned him as an authority, made his coaching offers more valuable, and eliminated the need to prove himself — his book did that for him.

Today, Daniel runs a thriving coaching business, speaks at major industry events, and is widely recognized beyond his corporate career.

And it all started with a book.

Your Book as a Multi-Purpose Asset

Most people think of a book as a book, resting on shelves, available in bookstores, or listed online. But its true power lies far beyond those places.

A book functions as a multi-purpose business asset. It builds client trust faster than any ad or sales pitch. It positions you as an authority event organizers want on their stage. It generates media and podcast interest simply by existing. It gives other industry leaders a reason to reach out, connect, and collaborate. And it signals to potential partners that you're someone serious — someone worth working with.

Here's what truly sets it apart:

Your book does this automatically.

Unlike ads or posts that fade, your book sticks around, making impressions long after it's published. It becomes your most memorable business card.

Real-World Examples: How Entrepreneurs & Professionals Leverage Their Books

Let's look at some real ways professionals have used their books to skyrocket their careers.

Connor was a business consultant. He was great at what he did, but he was struggling to stand out in a crowded industry.

He decided to write a book, not to sell copies, but to use it as a tool for his business.

He sent copies to potential clients, used the book as the anchor of his sales funnel, and leveraged it to justify higher consulting fees. The result: his closing rate skyrocketed. Clients came in already trusting his expertise, and he stopped having to convince anyone he was the right fit.

Case Study #2: The Coach Who Landed a TEDx Talk

Rachel was a leadership coach.

She had been trying to break into the speaking world for years, but she kept getting passed over.

Then she published her book.

The book got her first speaking invitation, then became her entry to a TEDx stage, then attracted higher-paid engagements she'd never previously been able to land. Before the book, she was another coach. After it, she was a thought leader — not because she'd suddenly become more qualified, but because she had something tangible that positioned her that way.

She hadn't suddenly become more qualified, she simply had something that positioned her as an expert in the eyes of event organizers.

Case Study #3: The Executive Who Used a Book to Build a Legacy

Lawrence had spent 30 years in the corporate world.

He wasn't trying to build a business, he wanted to write a book to share what he had learned and leave a lasting impact.

His book became a recommended resource inside his company, a mentoring tool for younger professionals, and a way to cement his legacy in his industry in a form that outlasted his career.

The book outlived his career.

Years later, people still reference it.

In contrast to fleeting social media content or temporary advertisements, a book spreads your message for years, potentially decades. It solidifies your legacy in a lasting format.

Case Study #4: Zig Ziglar – A Legacy That Lives On

Zig Ziglar built an empire on motivation, sales training, and leadership principles. But what truly cemented his legacy? His books.

Ziglar spent decades on stage, captivating audiences with his energy and wisdom. He coached thousands of sales professionals and business leaders, showing them how to achieve success with integrity and persistence.

But long after he passed away in 2012, his influence remains strong.

His books are still bestsellers. His lessons are still taught in leadership courses. His name still carries weight in sales and personal development.

Ziglar's books, like See You at the Top and Secrets of Closing the Sale, weren't business tools. They became timeless resources that still shape sales professionals and leaders today.

While Zig Ziglar's legacy was built over decades, the same principles apply today, whether you're a corporate leader, entrepreneur, or coach, your book can establish your credibility and continue working for you long after it's published.

This is what a book can do.

It outlives your career. It keeps spreading your message long after you're gone. It turns your life's work into something permanent.

For executives, thought leaders, and business owners, a book isn't about immediate results, it's about long-term impact. Whether you want to build a business today or leave a lasting contribution to your industry, your book will continue working for you for years to come.

Ziglar's name still matters because his books keep him relevant.

That's the power of publishing.

Why Ghostwriting Pays Off in the Long Run

If you're considering hiring a ghostwriter, you might be wondering:

Is it worth the investment?

Here's what you need to consider:

> The real return on investment isn't in book sales, it's in the business, branding, and career growth your book unlocks.

Let's break it down.

How a Book Pays for Itself Over Time

A ghostwriter is an investment.

Here's how your book can pay for itself (and more):

One speaking gig can cover the cost of ghostwriting. One high-ticket client can make the book worth it. One media feature can lead to new opportunities. One strategic partnership can open doors you never expected.

Most professionals make back their investment multiple times over.

Because a book isn't a one-time asset.

It keeps creating opportunities for years to come.

You now see how a book can transform your brand, your business, and your career.

But what happens if you don't take action?

The months add up. Every one that passes without your book in the world is a speaking gig that went to someone else, a client who chose the author over the expert, a media opportunity you weren't even considered for.

The difference?

Whether you decide to move forward or keep waiting.

Ghostwriting Is an Investment in Your Authority

At this point, it's clear that a book can unlock opportunities, drive business growth, and set the stage for sustained success. Beyond marketing and branding, however, lies an even more potent benefit: enhanced credibility.

A book doesn't put your name on a cover. It positions you as a thought leader. It makes investors, business partners, and high-level clients take you seriously. It turns your expertise into something tangible, something people can trust.

In the following chapter, we will delve into how a well-crafted book can solidify your authority, attract the right opportunities, and establish your reputation as an industry expert.

Creating a Book That Builds Credibility

There's a reason the most respected experts in any industry have written books. It's not about sharing knowledge. It's about establishing authority. In a world where credibility is currency, a book is the ultimate proof that you know what you're talking about.

Think about it. When you come across a professional who has published a book, you automatically assume they are an expert. Their ideas must be worth reading. Their insights must be valuable. Their voice must matter.

Now, imagine that professional is you.

A book changes the way people see you, and more importantly, the way they trust you. Whether you're seeking investment, board positions, high-ticket clients, or keynote speaking gigs, a book puts you in a different league, one where decision-makers take you seriously before you even step into the room.

It's not about writing words on a page. It's about owning the conversation, shaping industry discussions, and positioning yourself as the go-to authority.

Let's explore how publishing a book can elevate your credibility, attract serious business opportunities, and solidify your place as a leader in your field.

Your Book Is More Than a Book. It's Your Authority in Print

When Ethan pitched his startup to investors, he kept hearing the same thing: 'Interesting idea, but we're not convinced.' He knew his industry inside and out, but without a big name or track record, investors weren't biting.

So, he wrote a book. That decision changed everything. Almost overnight, the way people responded to him was completely different.

Investors saw him as an industry leader. His book became a credibility piece in pitch meetings. Venture capital firms started taking his calls.

The book didn't share his ideas, it positioned him as the expert who defined the conversation.

This is the power of a well-written book.

It doesn't tell people what you know, it proves you know it.

In this chapter, we'll explore how a book elevates your authority, attracts serious business opportunities, and solidifies your place as a leader in your field.

How a Book Establishes You as a Thought Leader

Think about the people in your industry who are known as leaders, experts, and go-to voices.

Now ask yourself: How many of them have written a book?

Chances are, most of them have.

That's because a book isn't a collection of ideas, it's a badge of credibility.

A book isn't a credibility booster, it's a business accelerator. Here's how publishing one instantly elevates your authority and attracts new opportunities:

It sets you apart from your competitors — many people talk about writing a book, but few actually do it, and that gap is your advantage. It gives you a platform, making it easier to land speaking gigs, media appearances, and partnership opportunities. It lets you control the conversation — instead of following industry trends, you become the source others cite. And it makes people take you seriously: a book is proof that you've put in the work to back up what you say.

When people see you've written a book, they assume one thing:

You know what you're talking about.

And in business, perception is often the difference between getting passed over and getting picked.

Attracting Business Partners and Investors Through Your Book

Many professionals write books for one reason:

To attract the right people — whether that's business partners, investors, or high-value clients.

Here's why it works:

Your Book Becomes a Trust-Building Tool

Before people do business with you, they want to trust you.

A book accelerates that trust.

Potential partners see your depth of knowledge. Investors recognize your expertise and vision. Your audience feels connected to you before you ever meet them.

Instead of trying to prove yourself in every conversation, your book does the heavy lifting for you.

Your Book Opens Doors to High-Level Connections

The right book attracts the right people.

A business leader reads your book and wants to work with you. An investor sees your insights and wants to hear your pitch. A major conference organizer decides you're exactly the speaker they need.

And the best part?

You don't have to chase these opportunities, they come to you.

Your book quietly does the talking for you, reinforcing your authority every time someone picks it up.

Commitment Signals Seriousness

Investors, partners, and high-value clients don't look for smart people.

They look for serious people.

When they see you've published a book, they recognize:

You're committed to your industry. You've taken the time to refine your knowledge. You understand the power of positioning.

And that makes you a much stronger choice for partnerships, investments, and long-term business growth.

Real-World Examples: Books That Opened Doors

Case Study #1: The Startup Founder Who Landed Venture Capital

When Alex launched his startup, he struggled to get in front of serious investors.

He had a great product, a strong team, and a clear vision, but he was unknown.

So, he wrote a book about the future of his industry.

Investors started reading it, it got him into the right rooms, and his book became a reference in pitch meetings.

Within six months of publishing, he secured a seven-figure investment.

Case Study #2: The Consultant Who Became an Industry Authority

Michelle had been a consultant for years, but she was always competing for clients.

She knew she was as good, if not better, than the "big names" in her industry.

But she needed a way to prove it.

So, she wrote a book showcasing her methodology and success stories.

Within a year, she doubled her rates. Her book led to keynote speaking invitations. She went from chasing clients to having them chase her.

Case Study #3: The Executive Who Used a Book to Transition to Board Memberships

After 25 years in the corporate world, Jason wanted to step into advisory roles.

But he needed something to make him stand out from the hundreds of other executives doing the same thing.

His book positioned him as an industry thought leader, led to multiple board invitations, and secured him high-paying advisory roles.

By writing a book, he cemented his legacy and opened new career opportunities, without having to "start over."

Why Your Book Is the Ultimate Business Card

A book is more than something you sell, it's something you leverage.

Instead of handing out business cards at networking events, imagine saying:

"I'd love to stay in touch. Here's a copy of my book."

It shifts the conversation.

Instead of claiming expertise, you've demonstrated it, on paper, in public, and on your own terms.

What Happens If You Don't Publish?

By now, you see how a book elevates your credibility and creates opportunities that wouldn't exist otherwise.

But what happens if you don't take action?

The authors who get there aren't necessarily the most qualified. They're the ones who acted first. Every month

you delay is another month someone with less experience
steps into the space your book should be occupying.

How to Find the Right Ghostwriter

Finding the wrong ghostwriter costs more than money. It costs time, trust, and often a manuscript you can't use. I've spoken to authors who went through two or three ghostwriters before they found the right fit — each false start setting them back months and draining the enthusiasm they started with. Getting this choice right the first time matters.

The Right Ghostwriter Makes All the Difference

By now, you know that writing a book can open doors, build your authority, and attract opportunities you never imagined.

But here's the truth:

You have the knowledge. You have the experience. You know your story needs to be told.

But turning that into a book? That's where people get stuck.

Maybe you've started writing but can't get past the first few chapters.

Maybe you've thought about hiring a ghostwriter but don't know how to choose the right one.

Or maybe you're afraid that a ghostwriter won't truly capture your voice.

The truth is the success of your book isn't about your ideas, it's about who helps bring them to life. A great ghostwriter doesn't put words on a page. They take what's in your head and turn it into a clear, compelling book that sounds like you, but at your absolute best.

A good ghostwriter doesn't write, they walk beside you, helping shape the messy middle into something meaningful. The wrong ghostwriter? That can leave you frustrated, stuck, and with a book that doesn't sound like you at all.

So how do you find the right ghostwriter?

In this chapter, you'll learn where to find the best ghostwriters, what to ask before hiring, and how to evaluate whether someone is the right fit. By the end, you'll know exactly how to choose the right partner for your book.

Where to Look for a Great Ghostwriter

That's exactly what happened to Nolan, a corporate executive who wanted to write a book to establish himself as an industry thought leader. He started by Googling "best ghostwriters" and quickly felt overwhelmed with thousands of results, but no way to tell who was qualified.

After wasting hours scrolling through freelance sites, Nolan decided to reach out to a colleague who had published a bestselling business book. *"I used a ghostwriter,*" his colleague admitted, "*and it was the best decision I ever made.*"

Nolan didn't find his ghostwriter on a search engine. He found them through a trusted recommendation. The result? A book that positioned him as a thought leader, led to speaking engagements, and opened doors to new business opportunities, all because he chose the right collaborator.

So where should you start your search?

Referrals are the gold standard — ask people who've published books you admire, because a strong recommendation from someone who's worked with a great ghostwriter carries real weight. Agencies like Gotham Ghostwriters and Kevin Anderson & Associates vet their writers for quality and cost more but provide peace of mind. Freelance platforms like LinkedIn and Upwork have independent ghostwriters, but quality varies and research is essential before committing.

Great ghostwriters aren't always easy to spot, but referrals and real conversations are often the fastest way to find someone you can trust.

The best ghostwriters are often found through word of mouth. If you know someone who has successfully published a book, ask them about their experience.

A great ghostwriter doesn't just write your book — they shape the entire experience. The right one makes what feels overwhelming become manageable, and makes collaboration feel natural rather than forced. They understand your vision, listen to your concerns, and stay engaged from the first conversation to the final page.

Who did they work with? Would they recommend them? A great ghostwriter will leave a lasting impression, not because of their writing, but because of how well they worked with their author.

Ghostwriting agencies curate and manage professional writers, ensuring quality and reliability. Some reputable agencies include:

Two of the most reputable agencies are Gotham Ghostwriters and Kevin Anderson & Associates.

Agencies often charge premium rates, but they provide quality assurance, vet their writers, and manage the entire process for you.

Freelance platforms like Upwork and LinkedIn can also help you find independent ghostwriters. These platforms allow you to browse profiles, read reviews, and see past work samples. However, quality varies widely, so due diligence is essential.

A word of caution: many writers on freelance platforms claim to be ghostwriters but have no experience writing a full-length book. Vet thoroughly before committing.

Language Fluency Matters

It might seem obvious, but it's often overlooked: your ghostwriter needs to be fluent in the language you're publishing in. Not conversational, professionally fluent. Grammar, tone, nuance, and idioms all shape how your message is received. A ghostwriter who struggles with those layers, even slightly, can leave your book feeling awkward or off-brand.

This becomes especially important if you're writing in English and considering international freelancers. Lower-cost writers can be tempting, but if their grasp of the language isn't strong enough to handle your voice, your credibility suffers.

Your ideas deserve to be expressed clearly and naturally. Make sure your ghostwriter has the command of language to do them justice.

Hiring the Wrong Ghostwriter is a Costly Mistake

Joe (not his real name) thought he was making the right decision. He needed a ghostwriter and found a "done-for-you" ghostwriting service that promised everything, fast turnaround, professional quality, and a price that seemed almost too good to be true.

Before signing, he called every reference they provided. The website looked great, but when he got on the phone, things didn't add up. Some past clients hesitated. Others had complaints about the process. It became clear that the service wasn't delivering what they promised.

Eventually, Joe reached out to a trusted professional for help.

I explained exactly what was happening. Their price was too low, which meant they were farming out the writing to multiple, underpaid freelancers.

The problems were exactly what you'd expect from a service farming work to underpaid freelancers: different sections of the book sounded like they were written by different people, the ideas were executed without care or depth, and instead of a smooth experience, Joe would have spent months fixing a manuscript that wasn't salvageable.

Joe scrapped his plan with the ghostwriting service and chose to work with me instead. And the result? A book that sounded like him, built his credibility, and helped him land multiple speaking engagements within months.

Joe almost wasted his time and money on a book that didn't sound like him. Now ask yourself, will you make the same mistake? Or will you choose a ghostwriter who understands your voice, your vision, and your goals?

Questions to Ask Before Hiring a Ghostwriter

Once you've found a potential ghostwriter, the real question is: Are they the right fit for you?

Imagine sitting down for your first call with a ghostwriter. You've read their work; you like their style, but can they bring your book to life? Here's how that conversation should go:

When you sit down with a potential ghostwriter, the conversation should flow naturally, like this:

"Can you share samples of books you've written?"

"Absolutely! Here are three books I've ghostwritten in your industry. Each has a distinct voice because every author is different."

"How do you make sure my book sounds like me?"

"Great question. I study your speaking style, past content, and interview transcripts. Then, I provide early drafts to fine-tune the voice before we go too far."

"How does your process work?"

"We start with a deep-dive strategy session, create a detailed outline together, and then I write in phases, so you're involved at every step."

By the end of this conversation, you should feel confident. More than that — you should feel excited.

"What's your timeline and availability?"

A full-length book typically takes 4 to 12 months to complete. Be upfront about your timeline and ensure the ghostwriter has availability to meet your needs. If they're overbooked or promise an unrealistically fast turnaround, proceed with caution.

Evaluating Compatibility, Expertise, and Process

Imagine meeting with your ghostwriter for the first time. You share your ideas, your goals, your vision. Do they lean in with curiosity? Do they ask the kinds of questions that make you think deeper? Do they seem as excited about your book as you are?

A great ghostwriter doesn't take notes.

They lean in.

They ask insightful questions.

They get excited about your ideas.

You trust someone with your ideas, your reputation, and your legacy. Beyond their writing ability, consider:

Personality and Communication

Hiring a ghostwriter isn't about skill; it's about trust.

Imagine sitting down with your ghostwriter every week for six months. Would you look forward to those conversations, or would they feel like a chore?

A great ghostwriter doesn't take notes, they lean in. They ask insightful questions. They get excited about your ideas. If your gut tells you there's something "off" about the dynamic, listen to that instinct.

The best ghostwriting partnerships don't feel like business transactions. They feel like collaborations where both of you are working toward the same goal, creating a book that changes lives.

Ghostwriting requires discipline, organization, and meeting deadlines. Look for signs of professionalism: Do they respond promptly? Do they outline clear next steps? A good ghostwriter should feel like a business partner, not a creative risk.

If a ghostwriter has a solid track record, they should have client testimonials or referrals. Check their background, read reviews, and ask for references if necessary. A history of repeat clients is a strong sign of quality work.

What Happens If You Hire the Wrong Ghostwriter?

Hiring the wrong ghostwriter can be a costly mistake. It can result in:

Hiring the wrong ghostwriter typically produces one of three outcomes: a book that doesn't sound like you, wasted time and money, or a drawn-out process that damages confidence in the project before it's even finished.

That's why due diligence matters. Take the time to find someone who aligns with your vision and understands your goals. When you do?

You get a book you're proud of, establish your authority in your field, and finally hold a finished book instead of an idea.

The Ghostwriting Interview: Where the Magic Begins

It all starts with the interview.

Some people assume ghostwriters disappear and return with a finished manuscript based on a few notes, but it's far more collaborative than that. The ghostwriting interview is where the magic truly begins. This is where all those scattered ideas finally start making sense, where your story starts to sound like you.

Let me introduce you to Sarah, a coach who wanted to write a book to boost her business. She came to me with a lot of ideas, but nothing concrete. At first, she wasn't sure what she wanted her book to accomplish. Was it a marketing tool? A legacy project? A way to solidify her authority in the coaching industry?

When Sarah sat down for our first interview, she was a bit overwhelmed. We spent a couple of hours talking about her work, her philosophy, and why she believed in her coaching methods. At first, it felt like we were having a conversation. But soon, as we dug deeper, her purpose for the book came into focus.

The Power of the Interview

In that first interview, I quickly realized it wasn't about listing facts or outlining chapters. It was about finding the heart of the book, through my own stories, struggles, and wins. Talking it through helped me hear my voice more clearly than I ever had before.

What surprised me most was how natural it felt. It wasn't some formal Q&A, it was more like someone truly listening. My tone, my energy, the way I explained things... it all started forming the foundation of the book. It was in that moment I knew this wasn't a writing project, it was a reflection of me.

Preparation Is Key

Preparation mattered, on both sides. Before the interview, I was encouraged to think through what I wanted the book to achieve. That meant reflecting on my own journey, identifying key themes, lessons learned, challenges I'd faced, and stories that still stood out to me. It wasn't always easy, but it helped me see how much I had to say.

When we met for the interview, my ghostwriter came in with thoughtful questions, not about what I do, but why I do it. Questions like:

The right interview questions go deep: what's the story behind your coaching journey, what do you want people to walk away with after reading your book, can you share a turning point in your career that shaped your philosophy, and how do you want your readers to feel after they've turned the last page?

They weren't the kind of questions you can answer on autopilot, they made me think in a whole new way. And as I answered them, I could feel the narrative taking shape.

Without that preparation and those conversations, the book wouldn't have the same depth, emotion, or authenticity.

Building Trust and Rapport

What surprised me most about the ghostwriting interview was how quickly trust became the foundation. I had to feel comfortable sharing not my achievements, but the messy moments too, the ones I usually gloss over. It felt a bit like handing someone the keys to a closet I hadn't opened in years. I expected judgment, but instead, they leaned in. Genuinely curious. It felt safe to share.

I wasn't sure what stories were "too much" or whether certain experiences were even relevant. But my ghostwriter made it clear, everything mattered. The tough lessons, the quiet wins, even the failures that still sting.

And as I opened up, something shifted. Those raw, real parts of my journey turned out to be the beating heart of the book. What I thought might make me look weak made the story stronger, more relatable, and more human.

Digging Deeper

Somewhere during the interview, things got unexpectedly real. At first, I was sharing surface-level stuff, my background, my approach, the usual talking points. But then the questions started digging deeper:

The deeper questions reveal the real material: what's the hardest part of your work that no one sees, how do you handle failure, and what do you wish someone had told you when you were starting out?

I hadn't prepared for those. And that's when it hit me, this book wasn't going to be a collection of tips or polished success stories.

As I talked through those tougher questions, I found myself telling the story of how I went from barely booking clients to building a thriving coaching business. I'd never shared that part in full before. In that moment, I realized it wasn't a side note, it was the heart of the book. That turning point, that struggle, became the message everything else would build around.

The Follow-Up

The interview didn't end when the call did. In many ways, that first conversation was the beginning. Afterward, my ghostwriter spent time reviewing everything we'd discussed and went through the materials I'd shared, things like old blog posts, speeches, and even testimonials from clients.

A few days later, we had a follow-up conversation. Then another. Each time, we peeled back another layer. Sometimes it was to clarify a story, other times it was to explore an idea that had come up in passing but turned out to be more important than I realized.

I didn't feel rushed. The process was thoughtful and intentional. And over time, it was like my book slowly took shape, my voice, my message, my perspective, reflected back at me with surprising clarity.

Your Story Matters

That initial conversation set the tone for everything that followed. It wasn't about facts, it was about discovering what mattered to me, understanding my story, and making sure that my voice came through with clarity and honesty.

For Sarah, the book we ended up creating was more than a business tool. It became a reflection of her journey, her struggles, and her triumphs. And when people read it, they didn't learn about her coaching philosophy, they connected with her as a person.

That's the power of ghostwriting done right. It's not about putting words on a page. It's about creating something real and authentic, something that will resonate with readers long after they've finished the last chapter.

The Ghostwriting Agreement: Setting the Stage for Success

> A contract doesn't kill creativity, it gives it the structure it needs to thrive.

When a client decides to work with a ghostwriter, the first crucial step is the contract. Think of it as the roadmap for the project, it defines the terms, the scope, and the expectations. Without a clear agreement, it's easy for things to get misaligned. What the client envisions and what the writer delivers can drift apart quickly. A solid ghostwriting agreement builds trust, defines boundaries, and sets the stage for a smooth, professional relationship.

The Beginner Ghostwriter

When Claire first launched her ghostwriting business, she was excited, hungry to build her portfolio, and ready to help people tell their stories. One of her first clients was a charismatic entrepreneur with a powerful life journey and dreams of publishing a book that would inspire millions. They clicked instantly. The client shared his vision, Claire captured it, no contract, no paperwork, raw enthusiasm.

It didn't take long for things to go wrong.

Claire delivered a few sample chapters, and at first, the client was thrilled, until he wasn't. Soon, he started asking for significant changes: different tone, different audience, entire sections scrapped and rewritten. The vision shifted weekly. He sent long, late-night voice notes with new ideas, and expected instant turnarounds. Six weeks in, he demanded more work... and then abruptly paused the project.

He wanted his deposit back.

Claire had nothing in writing, no agreement on scope, revision limits, or what "done" looked like. The client assumed she was his full-time writer on call. Claire assumed they were building a tight, focused book. Both were disappointed. The client walked away with partial drafts and frustration. Claire walked away unpaid, exhausted, and questioning whether she belonged in this business.

A few months later, Claire met a new client: Jason, who had a clear idea for a leadership book targeting young professionals. This time, she did things differently.

They started with a ghostwriting agreement.

They outlined everything: how many chapters, how many revisions, deadlines, payment schedule, and what would happen if the project needed to pause. It wasn't about being "legal", it was about being professional and protecting the working relationship.

That one document reshaped the entire experience.

When creative changes came up (and they always do), they simply revisited the contract. Expectations stayed clear. Claire didn't feel taken advantage of, and Jason didn't feel lost in the process. The book came together smoothly, on time, and with mutual respect. Jason was thrilled with the finished manuscript, and Claire finally experienced what it felt like to be paid well for great work, without the stress.

A contract isn't a formality, it's a foundation. Claire learned the hard way that skipping the agreement, no matter how "good" the vibe feels, can lead to disappointment and lost income. But with the right boundaries in place, ghostwriting becomes what it's meant to be: a creative partnership built on trust, clarity, and shared vision.

Why a Ghostwriting Contract Matters

It might look like legal stuff on paper, but a ghostwriting contract is what keeps both sides grounded when the unexpected happens. It's easy to think that everything will go smoothly, especially if you have a great relationship with the person you're working with. But in business, clarity is essential.

The contract should spell out scope of work — exactly what's included, from draft count to revision rounds — along with payment terms detailing whether it's hourly, by project, or milestone-based. It needs to address copyright and ownership, clarifying who holds the rights once the book is complete. A timeline section sets realistic deadlines so both parties stay on track, and a confidentiality clause ensures the ghostwriter won't share project details without permission.

When Jason signed the agreement, he and the ghostwriter felt much clearer about their roles and expectations. They knew the payment schedule, the deadlines, and the exact structure of how the book would unfold. No misunderstandings. No stress. Just a clear roadmap to success.

What Should the Ghostwriting Contract Include?

The agreement should clearly identify both parties by name and contact details. Scope of work defines exactly what's being delivered — chapters, research required, and whether the ghostwriter handles edits and revisions. Payment terms specify the structure, amounts, and due dates. A timeline covers each phase of the project. Ownership and copyright clarifies who holds the rights upon completion, a revisions clause specifies how many rounds are included, and a termination clause allows either party to exit under specific conditions.

The Key to a Successful Ghostwriting Partnership

That contract? It kept both sides from stepping on each other's toes. Expectations stayed clear, and no one had to guess what came next. When the details are spelled out early, it's easier to stay aligned, focused, and stress-free as the project moves forward. As Jason and Claire began working on his book, they had a solid foundation to build on. The contract became their compass, keeping the project on track from the first meeting to the final page.

One final note: if your book involves real, identifiable people or sensitive events, a brief consultation with a publishing attorney before you go to print is worth the investment. It takes an hour and can prevent significant headaches later.

Understanding Your Publishing Options

Before you start writing, you need to decide how your book will reach the world.

This isn't a last-minute decision, it's the foundation of your entire publishing strategy. The decision you make now affects your entire journey, how fast you publish, how much say you have, and even the way you write your book.

Too many authors wait until the end to figure this out. That's a mistake.

The wrong path can delay your book, limit your reach, or cost you more than you expected. But if you decide now, everything else, your writing, marketing, and launch strategy, will fall into place.

Choose wisely now, and you'll set yourself up for success from day one.

This isn't something you figure out at the end. Your publishing path influences everything: your timeline, your budget, your level of creative control, and even how you write the book itself.

Are you aiming for a major publisher and a book deal? That means refining your proposal early and understanding industry expectations. Do you want to self-publish and keep full control? Then you'll need to plan for editing, cover design, and distribution upfront. Is a hybrid publisher a better fit? That means factoring in the investment and researching reputable companies now. Or are you printing books yourself for events and clients? That changes everything about how you approach book production.

Too many authors leave this decision for last, only to realize they should have been preparing for their chosen path from the beginning. Don't make that mistake.

By the time you finish this chapter, you'll have a clear sense of which publishing route fits your goals, so that every step you take in writing and production leads to the result you want.

The Crossroads of Publishing

Emma had done everything right. She had built a thriving business, become a respected voice in her industry, and now, she had a book, almost.

She had spent months working with a ghostwriter, shaping her knowledge into something powerful. But now, faced with the publishing process, she felt lost.

Should she go the traditional route and try to land a big-name publisher? Take control and self-publish? Or was there a middle ground that offered the best of both worlds?

The deeper she looked, the more overwhelming it became. Some authors swore by traditional publishing for its credibility. Others had built empires through self-publishing. There were hybrid publishers promising the perfect balance, but they came with hefty price tags.

And then there were the horror stories, authors who waited years for a traditional deal that never came, those who self-published and sold only a handful of copies, and others who paid tens of thousands to a hybrid publisher only to realize they were on their own when it came to marketing.

Emma needed a clear answer: which publishing path was right for her?

Making the Right Choice for Your Book

Emma had four choices, and none of them were perfect.

Traditional publishing offered credibility but little control. Self-publishing gave full control but demanded effort. Hybrid publishing balanced support and ownership, but at a cost. Printing her own book was great for events but lacked scalability.

So, which one was right?

It came down to this:

What was her priority?

If she wanted prestige and didn't mind waiting, traditional was the answer. Full control quickly and willing to market it herself? Self-publishing. Professional help and able to invest? Hybrid. Just needed books for personal sales and events? Print herself.

How the Ghostwriting Process Works

You met Danielle earlier — the cybersecurity executive who walked into her first interview convinced her stories were too technical, too industry-specific, too niche. By the time the interview ended, she had her book: not a cybersecurity manual, but a wake-up call for business leaders who were unknowingly putting their companies at risk. A book that was entirely, unmistakably hers.

From Idea to Book. Without the Overwhelm

Aiko was used to being in control. As a corporate strategist in Tokyo, she spent her career solving complex problems, advising CEOs, and streamlining operations. But when it came to writing her book, she felt completely lost.

She knew her material. Her life was filled with lessons and insight. But turning those into a book others would want to read? That was unfamiliar territory.

Then she met her ghostwriter. Over tea in a quiet Shinjuku café, she explained her vision: why this book mattered, who it was for, and what she wanted readers to take away. Her ghostwriter listened, asked questions, and mapped out a clear process.

By the time they finished, Aiko felt something she hadn't expected, relief.

She wouldn't have to struggle through messy drafts, worry about sounding unnatural, or second-guess her structure — she could focus on her ideas while her ghostwriter shaped them into a professional, polished book.

A Note on Ghostwriting Styles: Not all ghostwriters follow the same process. Some offer highly collaborative experiences, working closely with you every step of the way. Others operate more independently, collecting information and returning with a full draft before you see a word.

Some ghostwriters conduct live interviews and write based on those conversations, while others prefer written input through notes, transcripts, or past content. Some send drafts chapter by chapter, while others deliver a nearly finished manuscript all at once.

Understanding these differences is critical when hiring a ghostwriter. If you want heavy involvement and regular feedback loops, you need someone with a collaborative approach. If you prefer to be hands-off and let an expert take the reins, a more independent ghostwriter might be a better fit.

Aiko's experience? A hybrid of both. She was involved in the vision and messaging but didn't have to do the heavy lifting of writing. She provided feedback, but her ghostwriter handled the execution.

Step 1: Discovery – Understanding the Vision

Before a single word was written, they focused on clarity.

Aiko's ghostwriter didn't start with writing. They started with questions, deep, thoughtful ones.

The discovery phase starts with three essential questions: what do you want this book to accomplish, who do you imagine reading it, and how do you want them to feel when they finish?

Aiko had never thought about her expertise this way before. But as she answered, her book started to take shape.

Together, they outlined her key message, the transformation she wanted for her readers, and the voice that felt most authentic to her.

Step 2: Outlining – Creating the Roadmap

Aiko had always believed in structure. A solid plan made execution effortless. The same applied to her book.

Before any writing began, her ghostwriter created a detailed outline. Chapter by chapter, they mapped out the flow, where stories would go, what concepts needed emphasis, and how everything connected.

For the first time, Aiko saw her book as something real, not an idea.

And best of all? Nothing moved forward without her approval.

Note: Some ghostwriters take a different approach. Instead of creating a full outline up front, they conduct in-depth interviews, then write the entire draft before presenting it for review. Others prefer to work in stages, drafting and refining chapter by chapter. The process can vary widely depending on the ghostwriter's style, the author preferences, and the book's complexity.

I prefer a more collaborative approach, outlining, drafting in sections, and refining as we go. This reduces the need for major revisions after the book is finished, ensuring a smoother process and a final product that truly reflects your voice and vision.

Step 3: Drafting – Writing Without the Struggle

Aiko's biggest fear was that her book wouldn't sound like her. That her personality, her way of thinking, would be lost in translation.

Instead, her ghostwriter captured her voice by talking with her, not writing for her.

They met regularly, recording conversations where she spoke naturally, telling stories, explaining ideas, sharing insights.

From those discussions, her ghostwriter crafted the first draft. When Aiko read it, she was stunned.

"This sounds exactly like me."

Every paragraph echoed her voice. The dry wit, the sharp edges, the way she taught through story, it was unmistakably her, only sharper.

Note: Great ghostwriting isn't about writing well, it's about disappearing into someone else's voice so completely that no one ever knows you were there. Great ghostwriters do more than write well, they capture the rhythm of how you think, speak, and connect with others. So when someone reads your book, it doesn't sound like you, it feels like you.

Step 4: Polishing – Making It Exceptional

The first draft was strong. But Aiko knew that in business, excellence is in the details.

The polishing stage covers professional editing to sharpen clarity, flow, and engagement; final structure checks to ensure everything connects seamlessly; and proofreading to fix typos, grammar, and consistency.

When she read the final version, she felt something she never expected, pride.

This was her book. Not her ideas, but her best ideas, presented in the strongest possible way.

Step 5: Publishing – Choosing the Right Path

With her manuscript complete, Aiko faced one last decision: how to publish.

Publishing options break into three paths: traditional publishing, a long but prestigious route requiring agents and publishers; hybrid publishing, a mix of control and professional support; and self-publishing, full ownership, full control, full responsibility.

She weighed her options carefully, knowing that the right choice depended on her goals.

Case Study: Doris's Dream Turned Into Reality

Let me tell you the story of Doris.

She came to me with thousands of pages of dream journals — decades of handwritten notes — and asked if I could turn them into a novel. I was intrigued. This wasn't a book idea, it was her life's work, captured in ink and memory.

So, we did it. We sifted through the notes, found the threads of a story, and shaped them into a novel. Her sister stepped in as an editor, helping to polish the manuscript. And then, the moment arrived.

When I handed Doris the finished copy of her book, I'll never forget the look on her face. She held it like something fragile, something precious.

Then she said, "This feels almost like when I held my first-born child in my hands a few minutes after she was born."

For some, a book is a business tool. For others, it's a personal milestone. But for people like Doris, a book isn't words on a page, it's the realization of something they've carried inside them for years, sometimes even a lifetime.

And that's why finding the right ghostwriter isn't about skill. It's about trust. About knowing that the person shaping your book will honor its meaning, capture its heart, and bring it to life in a way that feels as powerful as the story itself.

Why This Process Works

Most people who try to write a book alone never finish.

But Aiko? She did, without the struggle.

She didn't have to force herself to write — she simply shared her ideas. She didn't have to guess what to include — the outline made it clear. She didn't have to stress over every word — her ghostwriter refined and polished.

By the end, she had a book that captured her expertise, strengthened her brand, and positioned her as a thought leader.

And when she finally held the printed copy in her hands, she knew, this was one of the best investments she had ever made.

Building a Strong Ghostwriter Relationship

A great book doesn't come from hiring talent alone. It takes a real partnership built on trust and a shared vision. Ghostwriting only works when there's trust, clear communication, and a common goal between writer and client. After all, this is your story, and the ghostwriter's role is to bring it to life in a way that resonates with your audience.

Let me tell you about a client I'll call Angela. Angela's story was one of the most gut-wrenching I'd ever heard. At 14, her parents sold her to a pimp. She was forced into the sex trade, got hooked on drugs and alcohol, and stayed in that world for nearly 20 years.

But somewhere in the darkness, she found a way out, a Christian man who saw something in her no one else ever had. He helped her escape, get clean, and rebuild her life. Now, she's married, raising five kids, and wanted to tell her story, not for herself, but to help others like her.

When she came to me, she said, "I need to get this out. I need people to know what happened and what God did for me." We started strong.

In this chapter, we'll explore how to establish a strong, collaborative relationship with your ghostwriter, ensuring that you're both on the same page throughout the process. From setting expectations to maintaining open lines of communication, building a great working relationship is key to achieving a book that reflects your unique voice and vision.

This Is a Partnership, Not a One-Time Transaction

Writing a book with a ghostwriter is a long-term collaboration, not a transaction. It requires trust, open communication, and mutual respect. The words matter, but what matters more is making sure your vision comes through in every line — and that both parties feel heard throughout the process.

Let me tell you about Victor, a seasoned executive who wanted to write a book to showcase his leadership experiences and lessons. Victor was the hero of his own story: he had valuable insights to share with the world. But when he sat down to write his book, he hit a wall. His writing felt flat and didn't capture the energy of his ideas.

Victor needed a guide, a ghostwriter who could take his scattered thoughts and turn them into a cohesive, compelling narrative. Through his experience, he learned what it takes to build a strong, productive relationship with a ghostwriter. Here's what he learned, and what you can too.

For months, your ghostwriter will sit in the passenger seat of your journey, hearing your memories, your turning points, your truths. That means your working relationship matters as much as their writing ability.

When it's working well, the relationship doesn't feel forced. Both sides bring respect, energy, and a shared commitment to the book's success.

So, how do you build a strong relationship with your ghostwriter?

What Makes a Ghostwriter Relationship Work?

There are five things that make ghostwriting work: trust, clear communication, flexibility, shared vision, and professionalism.

Trust – Your Ghostwriter Has to "Get" You

Victor had the expertise and the stories. What he lacked was a way to share them authentically. When he hired a ghostwriter, he initially chose someone who seemed professional but didn't quite get his voice. The drafts felt off. They were polished, but they weren't Victor. His voice, his spark, the passion behind his leadership story, it wasn't there.

After multiple frustrating conversations, Victor hired someone new, someone who listened more deeply. This ghostwriter asked questions that unearthed Victor's values and helped shape the message behind his leadership style. It wasn't about transcribing his ideas; it was about helping Victor find clarity and structure in what he truly wanted to say.

Lesson learned: If your ghostwriter doesn't get you, that's a red flag. You need someone who truly understands your voice.

Key Element: The ghostwriter is your guide. They need to understand your story, your vision, and your values.

Victor learned the hard way that communication is critical. Early on, he thought he could "pass off" his ideas and let the ghostwriter work. But as drafts came in, he realized he had expectations that hadn't been clearly communicated.

He hit pause and reset the rhythm, they agreed on weekly check-ins, creating space to talk things through, not trade edits. He agreed to review drafts more actively. His new ghostwriter laid out timelines and communication protocols from day one, when to expect drafts, how to give feedback, and what would happen next. That structure calmed Victor's anxiety and kept the project moving without surprises.

Lesson learned: Clear communication is essential to keep the project on track. Make sure both you and your ghostwriter know how and when you'll communicate.

Key Element: Trust is built through open communication, and you should expect updates and feedback regularly.

Victor didn't always get things right the first time. At one point, he felt a section of the book wasn't hitting the mark. He wanted to add more personal stories to connect with the readers. His first ghostwriter resisted the change, claiming it would mess with the structure.

But with his new ghostwriter, the process was different. They had built a relationship where Victor felt comfortable giving feedback without fear of the writer rejecting it. They worked together to revise the section, making it feel more authentic to Victor's journey.

Lesson learned: Don't settle for a ghostwriter who can't take feedback. The right ghostwriter will be flexible, making necessary revisions to improve the book.

Key Element: A good ghostwriter expects feedback and is open to making revisions. They're here to support your vision.

Alignment – Your Vision Should Match Their Strengths

Victor needed a ghostwriter who could not only write well but who understood his leadership journey. His first ghostwriter had a great writing style, but they lacked the understanding of leadership and strategy that was essential to Victor's story.

He found a ghostwriter whose specialty was writing leadership books. They had worked with CEOs and executives, and they knew how to structure ideas in a way that positioned the author as a thought leader. The partnership flourished because the ghostwriter's strengths matched Victor's needs.

Lesson learned: Make sure the ghostwriter's strengths align with your vision. If you're telling a story about leadership, make sure they're experienced in that field.

Key Element: Your ghostwriter must align with your vision and be able to adapt to your style.

> ### *Professionalism – Your Ghostwriter Must Meet Deadlines and Deliver Quality*

Deadlines were a concern for Victor. When he first started working with a ghostwriter, the drafts came in late, and revisions took longer than expected. This lack of organization and follow-through left Victor frustrated and worried that his book wouldn't be done on time.

But with his new ghostwriter, deadlines were met. He received regular updates on the progress, and the quality of the writing exceeded expectations. Most importantly, Victor felt his book was a priority for the ghostwriter.

Lesson learned: Don't settle for someone who isn't organized or professional. A great ghostwriter respects your timeline and commitments.

Key Element: Professionalism is a must. Your ghostwriter should deliver quality work on time, every time.

Red Flags to Watch for When Hiring a Ghostwriter

Before you commit to working with a ghostwriter, watch for these warning signs:

Watch for these warning signs before you hire: a ghostwriter who doesn't ask good questions won't understand your vision. One who seems unwilling to adapt to your voice will impose their own style instead. If they're slow to respond before you even start working together, it only gets worse after. A good ghostwriter expects feedback and welcomes revisions — defensiveness is a red flag. If they can't articulate a clear process from idea to finished book, they likely don't have one. And if they're not genuinely excited about your project, the writing will show it.

How to Maintain a Strong Ghostwriter Relationship

Even after hiring, you want to keep the collaboration smooth and productive.

Articulate Your Expectations Clearly

Before work begins, align on a few things:

Agree on communication frequency — weekly updates, monthly calls, or something in between. Establish a clear feedback process: will you give written notes, talk through changes on video calls, or both? And nail down deadlines and deliverables so both sides always know what's expected and when.

This prevents misunderstandings and ensures you're always on the same page.

Give Honest, Constructive Feedback

Victor's journey was about learning how to provide effective feedback. Over time, he saw that clear notes made the book stronger, and helped his ghostwriter better understand his vision.

Lesson learned: Constructive feedback is essential. Your ghostwriter can't read your mind!

Victor's ghostwriter didn't write his book, they shaped it. There were times when Victor didn't understand why a certain change was necessary, but he trusted his ghostwriter's expertise. Their experience in writing for leaders like him helped refine his ideas and make the book even stronger.

Lesson learned: Respect the ghostwriter's experience. They're the guide, and they have insight into how to best craft the book you envision.

The Client's Key to Success

Victor's journey wasn't about hiring the right ghostwriter. It was about building a collaborative relationship where both sides contributed to the final product. His dedication to clear communication, timely feedback, and respecting the process made all the difference. Victor's experience made one thing crystal clear: the client isn't a participant, they're the engine. A great ghostwriter can drive, but only if the client provides the fuel.

As the client, you need to be actively involved, communicate clearly, and respect the process. When you do that, you set both yourself and your ghostwriter up for success. If you stay committed to the relationship, your book will reflect your vision and your voice, at its absolute best.

Great books are born from mutual respect. When both the client and ghostwriter bring their best, the story shines.

Final Thoughts: Building Your Book Together

A strong ghostwriter relationship isn't about handing off your book and disappearing. It's a collaborative process where your involvement shapes the final product. You and your ghostwriter will walk through the entire journey together, because the book you create will be a reflection of both your expertise and their skill.

Now that you know how to spot the right ghostwriter and what makes a strong collaboration, you can confidently choose the right partner for your book. The next step is understanding how to work together effectively to create your legacy.

What It's Like to Work with a Ghostwriter

When Danielle received the first draft of her introduction, she opened the document with her stomach tight. She'd been specific about her voice in the interviews — dry, direct, no jargon, no hype. She didn't want a book that sounded like a vendor. She wanted a book that sounded like her.

She read the first page. Then the second. Halfway through, she stopped. "This sounds exactly like me," she said. "Only sharper."

That's what a well-run ghostwriting collaboration produces. Not a book that sounds vaguely like you — a book that is you, at your most articulate. Here's what the process of getting there actually looks like from the inside.

It's a Collaboration, Not a Hand-Off

One of the biggest misconceptions about hiring a ghostwriter is that you pay someone, disappear, and magically receive a finished book.

That's not how it works.

A great ghostwriter doesn't replace you; they bring out your best ideas in a way that's clear, compelling, and structured.

Imagine hiring an architect to design your dream house.

You provide the vision, approve the plans, and have input on the details — but the expert handles the execution.

Working with a ghostwriter is much the same. You'll be involved at every step, but without the stress of writing every word yourself.

A Real Story: David's Journey

David, a corporate executive, had a wealth of knowledge and a powerful message to share. He dreamed of writing a book that would elevate his personal brand and establish him as a thought leader. But when he sat down to write, he quickly realized that putting his ideas into words was harder than he thought. After some frustration, he decided to hire a ghostwriter to help bring his book to life.

David soon realized that ghostwriting wasn't about handing over ideas. It was a dynamic, collaborative process that required him to be actively involved at key stages.

So, what can you expect from the process?

How Much Involvement Will You Have?

The level of involvement you'll have depends on a few factors:

The level of involvement is yours to define: do you already have a clear outline, or do you need help shaping your ideas? Do you want to be hands-on with every draft, or provide feedback at key milestones? Do you prefer regular check-ins, or do you want the ghostwriter working more independently?

In some cases, working with a client can be a smooth and collaborative process. However, there are times when things don't go as planned. For example, I once worked with a client who initially showed great enthusiasm for their book project.

We had a couple of one-hour interviews, and everything seemed to be progressing well. However, after those interviews, the client completely ghosted me, except to respond "proceed" occasionally to an email. I continued working on the manuscript, but communication was limited throughout the project.

This made the project extremely difficult, as I didn't have the feedback I needed to ensure the book truly reflected the client's voice and vision. While I still completed the book, it wasn't the most ideal collaboration, and it highlighted the importance of regular communication and active involvement from both parties in the ghostwriting process.

David chose a moderate level of involvement. He participated in in-depth interviews, approved the outline, and provided key feedback. From there, he let his ghostwriter take the lead, shaping the narrative while keeping David's voice intact. This level of collaboration allowed David to stay engaged in the process while not getting bogged down with writing every chapter himself.

How the Collaboration Works: Step by Step

Discovery & Vision Alignment

The first stage of working with a ghostwriter is about getting aligned.

This is when you discuss your goals, audience, and core message. The ghostwriter will ask detailed questions to understand your voice and perspective.

For David, this phase was essential. He didn't need someone to write for him; he needed someone who truly understood his vision.

At this stage, a good ghostwriter will get to know you as a person, how you explain things, and what makes your ideas unique. This ensures that when they start writing, it feels like you wrote it.

Outlining and Structuring the Book

Before diving into the writing, your ghostwriter will first create a detailed outline for your approval. This serves as the blueprint for your book, ensuring that everything is aligned with your vision before the writing begins.

A solid outline prevents the chaos of last-minute structural changes, wasted time, and disorganized content. For David, this stage was crucial. He reviewed the outline with his ghostwriter, ensuring everything that mattered was included. Once approved, the writing began.

Here's where the real magic happens.

Instead of staring at a blank page, you'll collaborate with your ghostwriter, sharing insights and discussing key ideas. They will then craft them into engaging, clear, and structured content that reflects your voice.

The collaboration flows through three stages: interviews and brainstorming where you answer questions, share insights, and discuss key points; drafting where the ghostwriter writes chapters based on your input; and review and feedback where you read through sections, suggest changes, and refine the content.

David went through several rounds of revisions, providing detailed feedback to ensure the chapters captured his message and tone. Sometimes, he'd ask for a section to be rewritten in a more conversational tone. Each time, his ghostwriter worked with him to refine the ideas, ensuring that David's voice came through clearly.

But as much as David gave feedback, he also trusted his ghostwriter's expertise, allowing them to take the lead on structure, tone, and flow. It wasn't about handing over all control; it was about working together to shape something that would resonate with his audience.

David's experience with his ghostwriter was a success because they communicated clearly, respected each other's expertise, and worked together as a team. Here are a few things you can do to ensure a smooth collaboration:

Set expectations early — David agreed to weekly check-ins that kept the process moving. Give constructive feedback: instead of "I don't like this chapter," say "This section feels too formal, can we make it more conversational?" And trust your ghostwriter's expertise — when they suggest cutting sections for clarity, it's in the book's best interest.

Red Flags That Signal a Bad Fit

Not all ghostwriter relationships are smooth. David's ghostwriting process was a success because they maintained open communication and mutual respect, but not all writers will be receptive to feedback or easy to work with.

Red flags in a working relationship include: lack of engagement or disinterest in your project, resistance to making changes or defensiveness when feedback is offered, drafts that don't sound like you and an inability to adjust, and missed deadlines or poor communication throughout.

David had a close call early in his search for a ghostwriter. He almost chose a service that seemed too good to be true, but after a few phone calls, he realized that their "promise" was too generic. Fortunately, he made the right choice, and the rest is history.

What Happens If the Collaboration Works Well?

When you and your ghostwriter are aligned, the process feels effortless.

You'll see your book come together faster than you expected. The content will sound like you, polished and professional. By the time your manuscript is complete, you'll feel assured that it reflects your message, captures your voice, and speaks directly to your audience.

And the best part?

The book will open doors, build authority, and work for you long after it's published.

Polish, Don't Perish: The Final Mile of Writing

John has spent the last year pouring his heart into his book. All those late nights, early mornings, and endless cups of coffee have finally paid off. His manuscript is done. The structure is in place. The words flow smoothly. But now, as he prepares to send his book out into the world, there's one final step: the revision pass.

John knows this is the final hurdle before launch. But now he's frozen, staring down the tunnel of endless edits.

He's ready to move forward, get his book published, and share it with readers. But how does he avoid revision hell?

Revisions Are About Refining, Not Reinventing

John's excited but nervous. The thought of rewriting sections makes him uneasy, especially after all the work he's put in. But here's the truth: the revision pass isn't about rewriting everything.

The heavy lifting is done. The story flows, the structure works. Now it's about smoothing the rough edges, not starting over.

John can't afford to get stuck. He's come too far. He doesn't need to redo everything; he needs to polish and perfect.

Avoid the Pitfall of Endless Rewriting

Many writers, John included, have heard the horror stories: authors who spent months, even years, rewriting and revising their books endlessly. They add, cut, and shuffle until the original story disappears.

John's not making that mistake. The revision pass isn't for tearing things apart, it's about refining what's already working.

He could still hear his ghostwriter's advice: "Your job now is to smooth things out, not rip them up."

John knows the revision process can be overwhelming, but he also knows it's essential to his success. He needs to stay focused on the right steps.

What Revisions Aren't For

John knows revisions are for polishing, not reworking. He knows it's just as important to understand what not to do as it is to know what to do. Here's what John doesn't want to get involved with during the revision pass:

Specifically: no rewriting major sections (the structure is already set), no adding new chapters (the content is locked), and no starting over (there's no need to rework

what's been created). The revision pass is for smoothing,
not rebuilding.

The key here is focus. John must resist the temptation
to stray from the course. He knows that each decision to
change something major will take him further from his
goal of publishing.

John's Revision Pass

Now that John knows what's at stake, he's ready to
focus and make these revisions count. His goal is clear: get
the book polished and ready for publication, not to
reinvent the wheel.

John has a clear plan for using his revision pass wisely:

The revision pass covers several types of refinement.
Clarifying sentences and tightening language makes the
writing clearer and more engaging. Correcting
inconsistencies — changed character names, mismatched
terms, formatting errors — ensures the manuscript feels
cohesive. Adjusting tone and voice fine-tunes sections that
feel too formal or too casual until the whole book sounds
like you. Catching gaps fills in missed transitions or
explanations that might confuse readers. And ensuring
smooth flow means each chapter leads naturally into the
next, keeping readers engaged from start to finish.

Maximizing the Revision Pass

Now that John knows how to focus his revision pass, he's ready to dive in. But first, he knows there are a few key steps to get the most out of the process.

Read the full manuscript first before revising any individual section — this gives you the full picture before you start changing anything. Be specific with your feedback: instead of "I don't like this section," say "This paragraph feels too formal — can we make it more conversational?" And stick to the agreed number of revision rounds — use them on the changes that actually matter most.

Why Extra Revisions Cost Extra

Once John reaches the agreed number of revisions, that's it. Any additional changes will require extra payment because it goes beyond the original scope. These changes will delay the publishing process and cost more money.

If John wants major changes beyond the scope of his revision pass, he'll need to have a conversation with his ghostwriter to discuss fair rates for the additional work.

Finalizing Your Book for Launch

When John finishes the revisions, he's pumped. The book is polished and ready for the editor. It's everything he envisioned, and more.

John knows revisions aren't about perfection, they're about making his book the best version of itself. He's made it to the final step, and now it's time to move forward.

What Happens After the Book is Written?

So, you've written the book. Congratulations! It's a major achievement, but the work isn't finished yet. The real challenge begins once your manuscript is complete. Publishing your book isn't the finish line, it's the start of something bigger. What you do with it afterward determines whether it sits on Amazon or becomes a door-opener for real opportunities.

In this chapter, we'll dive into the crucial steps that come after your book is written. From launching your book to using it as a marketing tool, this section will help you understand how to ensure your book continues to build your credibility, attract opportunities, and grow your brand. The journey doesn't end here; it's getting started.

The Journey Begins After the Last Page

When Jane hit "publish" on her book, she was excited. After all, writing and publishing a book is a monumental achievement, right? But as soon as she celebrated, she realized something: publishing is the starting point. It's the first step on a much bigger journey.

Her ghostwriter had always emphasized that a book isn't the finish line, it's the starting point. Now Jane had a book in her hands, but how was she going to leverage it?

How could she turn this achievement into something that would change her career?

The true power of your book comes from what you do with it after it's published.

> If you get your book into the right hands, it can open doors, new clients, partnerships, or speaking gigs. But it won't happen on its own.

Your book does more than tell your story, it keeps speaking for you when you're not in the room. Here's how to turn your book into the business asset you've always wanted.

Marketing Your Book – Getting It in Front of Readers

If no one knows about your book, all your hard work will go unnoticed. Jane quickly learned that publishing a book isn't enough. If you want it to drive sales, grow your business, and attract the right people, marketing is crucial.

The first 90 days are crucial. Why? Because Amazon's algorithm favors new releases, and media, podcasts, and reviewers are more likely to cover books that are new on the market. The earlier you start promoting, the better your long-term results.

What did Jane do immediately after publishing her book?

She emailed her network to let contacts, clients, colleagues, and friends know the book was available. She ran a launch discount, dropping the price to $0.99 to build momentum with fast sales and early reviews. She encouraged reviews by asking readers to share their thoughts on Amazon. And she did a social media push, sharing quotes, behind-the-scenes content, and feedback from early readers.

Pro Tip: The more activity your book gets in those first 30–90 days, the more Amazon will recommend it to new readers, increasing visibility.

Using Your Book to Land Speaking Gigs & Media Features

A book can be your golden ticket to the stage. Jane's ghostwriter had told her that authors are in high demand for speaking engagements because they've already demonstrated authority in their field.

A book is your credibility pass.

Jane used her book in several specific ways to boost her speaking career.

She added "author of [Your Book Title]" to her bio everywhere, instantly positioning herself as an expert. She sent free copies to event organizers to get her book in front of the right people. She repurposed book content into keynote speeches. And she created a speaker page on her website with the book as a central feature.

Pro Tip: If you want to speak at a specific event, send the organizer a copy of your book with a handwritten note. It's a personal touch that shows you mean business.

Jane didn't stop at speaking engagements. She used her book to land media features and podcast appearances as well:

Podcasts love interviewing authors, so she reached out to shows aligned with her book's message. She also submitted guest articles and press releases based on the book's content to magazines and online publications.

Pro Tip: Media features, like podcasts, remain online forever. A single appearance or article can keep driving traffic and sales for years.

Repurposing Your Book for Maximum Impact

Your book is not something to sell, it's content gold. Repurposing sections of your book can give you months (or even years) of marketing material. Jane used her book in a variety of ways:

She broke chapters into bite-sized blog posts and LinkedIn articles. She used the book as the foundation for paid speaking engagements and webinars. She created 60-second video clips summarizing key lessons for social media. And she turned one chapter into a downloadable lead magnet, offering it free for email sign-ups, then built an online course from the same material.

Pro Tip: You can get way more mileage from your book by reusing it, turn chapters into blog posts, talks, or video content your audience loves.

Beta Readers, Reviews, and Launch Teams That Work

You've got a finished book in your hands, or almost. The writing is done, the edits are locked, the formatting is finalized. Now what?

Many authors think the hard part is over once the manuscript is finished. But in truth, the last few steps, getting your book into readers' hands, can make or break your launch. And nothing helps more than social proof.

This final stretch is where your early readers and supporters can make all the difference.

Beta Readers: Your Secret Weapon for Last-Minute Polish

Before your book goes public, it should go private, to a small circle of trusted readers. These aren't editors or proofreaders. They're regular people (ideally in your target audience) who read the book in draft form and give you honest feedback.

Why beta readers matter:

Beta readers flag confusion, pacing issues, or moments that fall flat. They give you real-world reader reactions before the masses see it. And they help you ensure your book resonates beyond your own perspective.

Who to ask:

Look for ideal readers who match your book's target market, trusted colleagues or clients, members of your email list or online community, and past readers who've supported your work.

What to ask for:

Ask them direct questions: were there any parts that felt unclear or slow, did anything pull you out of the experience, which sections were most memorable or valuable, and if you could change one thing, what would it be?

Set a clear deadline and offer a quick way for them to respond, like a Google Doc with guiding questions. You're looking for honest impressions, not grammar notes.

Amazon Reviews: The Credibility Currency

Once your book is live, the most powerful asset isn't ads or SEO, it's reviews.

Why Amazon reviews matter:

Amazon reviews boost your visibility in the algorithm, provide social proof that your book is worth reading, and influence buying decisions more than almost anything else.

Amazon's own research shows that books with 25+ reviews dramatically outperform those with under 10.

Your goal? Hit that 25-review mark within 30 days of launch.

How to get them (without breaking rules):

Ask your beta readers to leave an honest review, build a launch team, follow up with everyone who received an advance copy, and include a review request in the back of the book itself.

What NOT to do:

Make it as easy as possible for them. Share a direct review link and let them know a simple sentence or two is all it takes to make a big difference.

Launch Teams: Your Word-of-Mouth Engine

A launch team (or street team) is a group of supporters who commit to helping you promote the book during your launch window. They're volunteers, friends, fans, colleagues, or readers who want to see your message succeed.

What a launch team does:

Each launch team member should leave a review on launch day, share the book on social media or in newsletters, join your launch events, and download early if you're offering a Kindle promo rate.

How to run a launch team:

Recruit via email, social posts, or personal invites. Communicate regularly with three to five clear updates and instructions. Equip them with promo graphics, sample posts, and links. And celebrate them publicly — thank them, share their content, tag them in posts.

You can create a private Facebook group or Slack channel for launch week energy. People love being part of something meaningful.

Other Final Touches That Drive Discovery

Editorial reviews from bloggers, influencers, or industry leaders give you blurbs for your Amazon page and website. Podcast and media appearances lined up around launch week multiply your touchpoints. An email list announcement shares your story, the book's promise, and a buy link. And a virtual launch party via Zoom or LinkedIn Live lets you share behind-the-scenes stories, answer questions, and invite people to get their copy.

The End of the Writing – Wrapping It Up the Right Way

Finishing a book is no small feat. After months of interviews, drafts, feedback, and revisions, there's finally a full manuscript sitting in front of you. You'll want to exhale and move on, but a few small steps at the end can save you from headaches later.

Writing a Testimonial (If You're Happy)

If your ghostwriter delivered what you hoped for, or better, it's a thoughtful and helpful gesture to write a testimonial. You don't have to say they "wrote the book for you" if that feels awkward. Many clients refer to their ghostwriter as a "writing coach," "editor," or "creative advisor." That keeps things professional and gives you flexibility in how much of the process you want to reveal publicly.

Sharing your experience gives future clients a glimpse into the process, and it's one of the best ways to thank the person who helped bring your book to life.

Revision Hell: Don't Get Stuck

Revisions are where many projects stall. One or two rounds of changes? Expected. Helpful, even. But too many authors fall into the trap of endless tweaks, changing names, adjusting timelines, or second-guessing entire chapters long after the writing is done.

> *I once had a memoir client who kept coming back with tiny changes, swapping out names, changing the setting of a childhood story, rethinking how he wanted to describe a key event. Every time we locked a chapter, he'd remember something else. It went on for weeks. Finally, I had to say, "We're past the revision phase. If we keep going, we need a new agreement."*

He wasn't being difficult, he couldn't let go. That's common. But at some point, you have to trust the work and call it finished.

Agree on how many revision rounds are included from the start, then stick to it. When that final pass is done, trust the process and move on.

Stay in Scope: What the Ghostwriter Does (and Doesn't)

Ghostwriters handle the writing. They take your ideas and turn them into a well-structured manuscript. But they're not publishers, marketers, or formatters. Unless your agreement specifically includes things like uploading to Amazon, designing the cover, or managing your launch, don't assume those things are included.

Some ghostwriters offer those services or can connect you with people who do, but that's a separate conversation.

Stick to what was agreed upon, and if you need more support, ask. Don't assume your ghostwriter is also your publisher.

Don't Disappear

If the manuscript is done, don't go silent. The final phase works best when there's clear communication. Your ghostwriter wants closure as much as you do. Wrap things up cleanly, with a final sign-off or approval, so everyone knows the job is finished.

Final Thoughts

Ending a book project can be emotional. You've spent time and energy bringing your story or ideas to life. It's natural to want every last sentence to be perfect, but chasing perfect will only delay your launch. At some point, good enough is great enough.

Finish strong. Offer a testimonial if the experience was good. Keep revision rounds under control. Respect the scope of the agreement. And most of all, take a moment to recognize what you've created.

Your book is finished. That's something worth celebrating.

Why Editing Matters – And Why Your Ghostwriter Shouldn't Do It

Note: If your book is to be traditionally or hybrid published, you will not need to hire an editor. This is handled by the publisher.

By the time your manuscript is finished, you're probably thinking, "It's done!" But there's one more critical step before it's ready for the world: professional editing. This is where a lot of authors drop the ball, and where a great book can still fall apart.

Let's get one thing clear: your ghostwriter is not your editor. Even the best ghostwriters shouldn't edit their own work. Why? Because they're too close to the manuscript. They know what the sentences are supposed to say. They've spent weeks, sometimes months, living inside your ideas and your voice. That familiarity makes it nearly impossible to spot errors, inconsistencies, or awkward phrasing.

Editing goes far beyond catching typos. Each stage fine-tunes your message, strengthens your voice, and ensures your book feels like it belongs on a shelf.

The Full Editing Suite: What You Really Need

Here's what a complete editing process looks like and why each stage matters:

Developmental Editing

The three core questions an editor brings to every manuscript: is the message clear and coherent, are the chapters arranged in a logical order, and does the book deliver on its promise to the reader?

It's the moment where you step back and ask, does this house even have the right rooms? Before you hang the pictures, make sure the walls are in the right place.

Line Editing

Once the structure is solid, a line editor gets granular. This level focuses on sentence structure, word choice, rhythm, and overall readability. It's about making sure your voice shines without clunky phrasing or redundancy. They smooth out the language without changing the meaning.

Copyediting

Copyediting is where things get technical. Grammar, punctuation, and sentence mechanics take center stage. A sharp copyeditor will clean up the messiness you didn't even realize was there, like a comma in the wrong spot that changes your tone.

The final polish. A proofreader catches surface-level errors before printing or publishing, things like typos, formatting issues, and spacing problems that even experienced editors might miss during earlier passes. This is your last line of defense before it goes to readers.

Every stage matters, except developmental editing, which is only necessary if the manuscript requires major structural work. Skip one, and your book might come off rushed or unfinished.

When to Bring in an Editor

Once your ghostwriter has delivered the final approved manuscript, including all revisions, it's time to bring in a professional editor. Don't begin editing while you're still making content changes. You'll waste time and money re-editing sections that may get rewritten anyway.

Hire your editor after the writing is done, but well before you plan to publish. Build in time for each stage. Developmental edits can take a few weeks, and the rest may add another month or more depending on your schedule and the complexity of your book.

Why Ghostwriters Shouldn't Edit Their Own Work

I once had a client ask, "You wrote it, can't you edit it too?" I get it, it sounds efficient. But it's a little like asking your architect to inspect the plumbing. Even if they could, they shouldn't. Writing and editing are two different crafts. Writers build the house; editors check for cracks, leaks, and load-bearing structure.

Ghostwriters are experts at drawing out your story and shaping your voice, but they're too close to it to see the cracks. That's what editing is for. They've spent too much time in the weeds to see the bigger picture. That's exactly what an editor brings: fresh eyes and detachment.

I've worked on dozens of manuscripts, and even when I write my own material, I hand it off to an editor. We all need that second set of eyes, no matter how experienced we are.

Why AI is Not a Replacement for Human Editors

Sure, AI tools are fast and convenient, and they're getting better all the time. But handing your book over to a machine and calling it "done"? That's a shortcut that'll show.

Not if you want a high-quality book.

AI tools are helpful for catching typos, flagging passive constructions, and identifying repetitive phrasing. But they can't understand nuance, tone, or context the way a human editor can. They don't understand your voice, your brand, or your goals, and they certainly don't know when breaking the rules makes your writing stronger.

I've seen manuscripts butchered by AI: edits that flatten the voice, strip out emotion, or rephrase sentences into robotic-sounding jargon. It's efficient, yes, but soulless.

AI also doesn't understand your reader. It doesn't know how to shape a message for impact or tighten a story for emotional resonance. It won't challenge your assumptions or catch gaps in logic, things that require real understanding and insight. That's what a good editor does. That's what makes the difference between a competent book and a powerful one.

Let AI help you catch surface-level stuff, but don't expect it to understand your story. For that, you need human eyes and heart.

Once editing is complete, your manuscript needs to be formatted for publication. For print books, use IngramSpark or a professional formatter with proper margins, headers, and trim size. For ebooks, ensure clean reflowable text without manual page breaks. Tools like Vellum handle both formats cleanly. If your book includes images or complex layout, hire a book designer.

Getting Your Book Published: Self, Traditional, Hybrid, and Audio

Once your manuscript is complete, the next decision is how to get it into readers' hands. There are four main paths: self-publishing, traditional publishing, hybrid publishing, and audiobook production. Each involves different tradeoffs of cost, control, speed, and reach. Here's what each one looks like in practice.

Self-Publishing

Self-publishing gives you full control over your book — timeline, design, pricing, and royalties. There are no gatekeepers, but there are real responsibilities: you cover editing, cover design, formatting, and promotion yourself. Done well, a self-published book can look and sell as well as anything traditionally published. Done poorly, it signals amateur work before anyone reads the first page.

US authors purchase ISBNs through Bowker at myidentifiers.com. Canadian authors receive them free through ISBN Canada. UK authors can buy through the Nielsen ISBN Agency.

One note on ISBNs: if you use Amazon's free ISBN, Amazon is listed as the publisher and you can't distribute elsewhere. Buying your own from Bowker gives you full control over distribution across all retailers.

The Traditional Path

Traditional publishing offers the most credibility and the least control. A publisher handles editing, design, distribution, and some marketing — but getting there requires a literary agent, a compelling proposal, and patience. The process from query to bookstore shelf typically takes two to three years.

The publisher's editing process moves through three stages: developmental editing for big-picture clarity and flow, copyediting for grammar, style, and consistency, and proofreading as a final polish before printing.

You'll have input on the manuscript, but the publisher makes final calls on title, cover, and edits. Most authors find the editorial process valuable — but come in expecting collaboration, not full control.

The Hybrid Model

Hybrid publishing sits between the two: you pay upfront for professional editing, design, and distribution support, but keep your rights and earn higher royalties than traditional deals offer. A reputable hybrid publisher curates submissions, maintains editorial standards, and distributes through Ingram to bookstores and libraries. The tradeoff is a real upfront investment — typically $5,000–$25,000 — in exchange for a faster timeline and more control than traditional publishing allows.

The Audiobook Advantage

When Julia finished her book, a powerful blend of leadership lessons and personal stories, she thought she was done. She had a print copy in hand, the Kindle version already live, and a few podcast interviews scheduled for launch week. But during a virtual book club appearance, someone asked, "Is there an audiobook version? I only listen during my commute."

That question stopped her. She hadn't planned on recording one.

But over the next few weeks, she heard it again and again. Her peers, her clients, even her own sister confessed they rarely had time to sit down and read. "I listen to everything while I walk the dog," one person told her. "It's how I finish books now."

That's when it clicked: her message might be reaching shelves, but it wasn't reaching ears. And ears, it turned out, were where the audience was listening.

Why Audiobooks Reach Deeper

Julia hadn't realized how many people lived by their earbuds. For them, audiobooks weren't a preference, they were the only way to get through a book. Whether it's a long drive, early morning walk, or winding down at night, audio fits into the nooks and crannies of daily life in a way that print can't. And while Julia had assumed her book was complete, she realized there was a whole group of readers she was unintentionally leaving behind.

That group wasn't small. Audiobook sales had been rising for years, far outpacing growth in print or digital. And it wasn't novels. Business books, memoirs, how-to guides, listeners were hungry for content that sounded like a personal conversation.

For Julia, that meant a choice: should she narrate it herself or hire someone else?

Should You Use Your Own Voice?

At first, the idea of narrating the book felt exciting. Julia had done some public speaking, and the idea of speaking directly to her audience gave her goosebumps. But then she tried recording a sample on her laptop, and after twenty minutes of fumbling through takes, background noise, and dry mouth, she wasn't so sure.

She asked around and got two pieces of advice she didn't expect to hear at the same time: "Your voice makes it personal," one colleague said. "But if you're going to do it, do it professionally."

And that was the turning point. She found a producer through a friend, booked a quiet local studio, and recorded her book over the course of a few afternoons. It was tiring, much harder than she expected, but also deeply satisfying. For the first time, she felt like she was reading the book to someone, not at them.

That tone, that intimacy, became one of her book's biggest assets.

Other authors choose to hire professional narrators, and that's a smart path too, especially for those who aren't comfortable in front of a mic or don't have time for studio work. A great narrator can bring nuance, polish, and consistency to your book. But if the story is deeply personal, or if your audience expects to hear you, then your voice may be the thing that builds trust.

Production Without the Headache

Julia quickly learned that recording was one part of the process. There was editing, mastering, file formatting, all terms she hadn't thought about until her producer brought them up. But that's the beauty of working with someone who knows the path. He cleaned up her recordings, adjusted the levels, added chapter markers, and made sure the files met the exact requirements for Audible and Apple Books.

The technical side was invisible to the listener, but absolutely vital behind the scenes. Without professional help, she never would've known what to submit or how to pass quality checks. And she was glad she didn't try to Google her way through it.

Distribution That Goes Beyond Amazon

With her files complete, Julia uploaded through a platform called Findaway Voices. It pushed her audiobook not to Audible, but to over 40 retailers, including Spotify, Google Play, and international stores she'd never heard of.

That was another lightbulb moment, her book didn't sound better in audio. It traveled farther.

She could have chosen ACX (Amazon's distribution arm), but their contracts were more restrictive, locking her into exclusive deals. Findaway gave her more control and a wider reach, and that aligned with everything she believed as an independent author.

She treated the audiobook as a second launch. New emails. Fresh posts. She even offered a bonus audio clip, deleted scenes, almost, for people who downloaded it in the first week. That campaign brought in new listeners who hadn't touched the print version.

Marketing Your Book: Turning Words into Business

Finishing a book feels like crossing a finish line, but it's actually the starting gate. Getting it into the hands of readers takes strategy and consistency. Even the best-written books disappear without a marketing plan. Here's how to make sure yours doesn't.

Before the Launch: Building Anticipation

One of the biggest mistakes authors make is waiting until their book is published to start thinking about marketing. The truth is, book marketing should start the moment you begin writing. Building anticipation is one of the most powerful ways to ensure that your book has a ready-made audience on launch day.

Create a website or Landing Page for Your Book

A dedicated landing page is a must-have for any author. Your website or page should include:

Your launch website needs a compelling book description, an author bio that builds credibility and trust, an email sign-up form for early subscribers, pre-order options or retailer links, and social proof like testimonials or quotes from early readers if available.

Having a landing page helps potential readers find more information about your book and allows you to build an email list of people who are excited for its release.

Start a Blog or Content Series

Creating content related to the themes of your book will help you build your personal brand and attract readers even before your book is available. Share articles, blog posts, or videos that dive into the ideas you explore in your book. Doing this not only builds authority in your niche, but it also helps potential readers feel more connected to your content.

By sharing snippets, insights, or even excerpts from your book, you can start to build excitement around the book's release. This content also positions you as an expert, as an authority in your niche.

Leverage Social Media

Don't wait until launch day, start building connections now. Share what's surprising you during the writing process. Post a quote you rewrote five times. Let people see the messy, human side of creating a book. Here are a few ideas:

Pre-launch social content should include teaser posts with an intriguing passage or quote, a dedicated hashtag people can follow and use, author milestone updates like finishing the manuscript or holding the first printed copy, and podcast or interview appearances where you discuss the upcoming book.

These efforts will help build an audience who is eager to buy your book when it's released.

Launch Day: Making a Splash

Your book's launch is critical, and it's all about making a big splash. With careful planning and a bit of creativity, you can get your book into the hands of your audience.

Create a Launch Plan

A successful book launch needs a strategic plan. This is not about sending out a press release; it's about organizing a series of events and activities to promote your book over several days or weeks. Here are some launch strategies:

On launch day, run giveaways to incentivize purchases and reviews, offer a limited-time free chapter download to generate interest, host a live event on Instagram, Facebook, or LinkedIn where you interact with your audience, and set up an online book tour with blogs, podcasts, and influencers in your field.

Influencer Marketing

Influencers can help you reach a broader audience. Whether they are people in your industry, niche influencers, or popular book reviewers, their endorsement can lend credibility and bring attention to your book.

Reach out to influencers with a free copy in exchange for an honest review or mention, and gather testimonials from respected figures in your field — a strong endorsement can significantly influence whether readers buy.

Make sure your email subscribers are the first to know when the book is available. Send out an announcement email with a link to buy the book and special incentives like limited-time discounts. Follow up with thank you emails to those who buy, and encourage them to leave reviews or share the book with their network.

Blog Tours: Expand Your Reach with Online Book Tours

A blog tour is an excellent way to create buzz and get your book in front of a larger audience. During a blog tour, you partner with several bloggers or content creators who will review or feature your book on their platforms. Here's how to get started:

A blog tour starts with identifying bloggers, reviewers, and influencers whose audiences align with your book's themes. Beyond a standard review, offer value-added content: guest posts on relevant topics, interviews where the blogger asks about your process, or excerpts that let potential readers sample your writing style. Then build a clear schedule of which blogs will feature your book and on which dates, coordinating with each blogger in advance so they have everything they need.

After the Launch: Sustaining Momentum

Once the book is out, the work isn't over. In fact, this is when the real magic happens, because you need to keep the momentum going long after the initial launch excitement fades.

Leverage Your Book for Lead Generation

Your book can do more than sit on a shelf. Done right, it becomes a door-opener, sparking new conversations, drawing clients in, and anchoring your authority. Use it as a lead magnet for new clients.

After launch, offer a free consultation or valuable resource to people who buy the book. Embed calls-to-action that drive readers to your website or email list. And use the book to attract speaking opportunities, guest podcast spots, and media appearances.

Create a Long-Term Marketing Strategy

Book marketing is a marathon, not a sprint. Continue sharing valuable content related to your book over time:

Sustain momentum by repurposing book content into blog posts, social media updates, or a podcast series. Run ongoing promotions and price discounts or bundle the book with your services. And track what's working — adjust your marketing efforts based on what's actually driving results.

Getting Your Book into Libraries and Bookstores

Publishing on Amazon gets you on the map, but it's far from the full territory. If you're serious about impact, visibility, and long-term credibility, you need to go beyond the algorithm. That means getting your book into libraries and bookstores, two places that operate on entirely different rules but can open doors Amazon never will.

These spaces are curated. Respected. Local. They introduce you to readers who don't browse online but do browse shelves. And unlike the click-and-scroll model of digital marketplaces, libraries and bookstores work through relationships, distribution systems, and reputation.

So, if you want your book to live a long and meaningful life out in the world, this is the chapter you've been waiting for.

Why Bookstores Still Matter

There's something powerful about seeing your book on a physical shelf. It isn't visibility, it's validation. Bookstores, especially independent ones, build community. They carefully choose what to carry. When your book is among their selections, readers assume it passed a kind of test, and that perception builds instant credibility.

Bookstores attract browsing readers who are open to discovery — not search-driven buyers who already know what they want. Being on a shelf means your book is available immediately. And in-person events like signings, launches, and local author nights are still one of the best ways to build a loyal audience.

When you walk into your local bookstore and see your book next to authors you've long admired, you realize: this isn't self-publishing. It's publishing, period.

Why Libraries Are a Hidden Goldmine

Libraries aren't quiet places full of books. They are trusted, respected institutions, and for many readers, they're the first place they discover new authors.

Librarians curate with intention. Librarians notice books that speak to their patrons' lives, topics like mental health, personal growth, leadership, or grief resonate deeply. And here's what most authors don't realize: libraries pay for your book.

Libraries purchase physical and digital copies through systems like OverDrive, Hoopla, and Baker & Taylor. If your ebook is licensed, you get paid per checkout — and it adds up. Libraries may also buy multiple copies if demand is high or you're doing a talk in their space.

More than sales, though, libraries build trust. If your book is in the stacks, it's considered valuable, reliable, and worth recommending. And that's not good for your ego, it's good for your brand.

The Platform That Gets You There: Draft2Digital

Amazon was never designed with libraries or bookstores in mind. Its "expanded distribution" sounds good, but rarely lands your book where it counts, and many bookstores won't stock Amazon-published titles. So, if you're hoping to get into either world, you need a different route.

Draft2Digital is a powerful, user-friendly platform that distributes your book to dozens of library and retail networks, without you needing to master the tech or pay upfront. It connects to:

Draft2Digital reaches OverDrive, Hoopla, BorrowBox, and Bibliotheca for library ebooks; Ingram for print distribution to bookstores; and Apple Books, Kobo, and Barnes & Noble for wider ebook retail.

Unlike IngramSpark, D2D doesn't charge setup fees, making it ideal for most authors. You can still publish on Amazon separately, but Draft2Digital becomes your library and bookstore engine.

And if you're serious about being taken seriously? Use your own ISBN. It helps you look like a legitimate publisher instead of just another Amazon author.

Getting On the Radar (It's a Strategy, Not a Hope)

Libraries and bookstores don't go looking for your book, you (or your team) have to introduce it to them. That starts with three things:

Getting into bookstores and libraries requires professional design and formatting, discoverability in the right systems including Ingram, OverDrive, and Baker & Taylor, and a sell sheet — your book's one-page resume — with the title, ISBNs, short pitch, audience, distribution details, and why it matters.

The real key? Consistent outreach. Too many authors send a few emails, hear crickets, and walk away. That's where persistence wins. But success here often comes from follow-up, personalization, and patience. Libraries and bookstores aren't in a rush, but they're always building their collections.

You Don't Have to Do This Alone

Hiring a virtual assistant (VA) or a freelance book publicist can help you scale this outreach without draining your time. A good assistant can:

A VA or marketing assistant can research local bookstores and library networks, send customized pitches and follow up, track responses and request purchases, coordinate local signings, readings, and panels, and submit your book to IndieBound and regional author catalogs.

You're still in control, but you're no longer doing it all yourself. You're not the writer, you're running the business behind the book.

Understanding the Cost of Ghostwriting – What You're Really Paying For

The most common moment in a first call with a prospective client is a pause. I've quoted the project. There's a beat of silence. Then: "That's more than I expected."

I had one client — a leadership consultant named Teresa — who had this exact reaction. She'd budgeted $8,000. My quote was $42,000. She thanked me for my time and said she'd think about it. Three weeks later she called back. She'd found a ghostwriter on Fiverr for $1,200, signed the contract, and received a first draft that read, in her words, "like it was written by someone who had never met me and had only read a Wikipedia summary of my industry." She was back at my door. We started over. She paid twice.

I'm not telling that story to be unkind about cheap ghostwriters. I'm telling it because it's the most common trajectory I see, and it's entirely preventable. Understanding what you're actually paying for — and what the real cost of the alternatives is — changes how you make the decision.

An Investment in Your Authority, Not Just Words on a Page

You have a story and message that can transform your career, business, or legacy. When hiring a ghostwriter, you'll soon realize: quality ghostwriting comes at a price.

That's when doubt creeps in. You wonder, "Why does it cost so much? Is it worth the investment?"

When you hire a ghostwriter, you're investing in a process that translates your thoughts into a well-structured, engaging book that reflects your expertise. It's not about writing, it's about creating a book that serves as a strategic tool for attracting clients, landing speaking gigs, and building your credibility.

It's the difference between scribbling blueprints on a napkin and working with someone who can take your vision and build a livable, lasting home, complete with the small touches you didn't even know you wanted. You wouldn't hand them some bricks and expect them to create a masterpiece without blueprints, a plan, and careful execution.

For a book to be successful, it requires a well-organized framework, smooth progression, and meticulous attention to detail. That's what a ghostwriter brings to the table, not words, but a carefully crafted tool that works for you.

Hiring a ghostwriter is about more than filling pages, it's about building a tool that opens doors, starts conversations, and represents the best version of your ideas.

The right question isn't "can I afford a ghostwriter?" It's "what does it cost me not to have this book?" Lost speaking opportunities, clients who went with the author instead, the years of compounding advantage your competitors are building right now.

What's the real impact you want your book to have on your business? Are you looking for recognition, new clients, or to cement your position as an expert? Your ghostwriter will help you craft a book that aligns with those goals.

Imagine attending a networking event where everyone already knows who you are, because they've read your book. You're no longer another expert in the field; you've become the authority. This is the power of a professionally crafted book. With the right ghostwriter, your message will resonate, building your credibility and positioning you at the forefront of your industry.

Why Ghostwriting Costs What It Does

At first glance, ghostwriting might seem like simple writing, but it's anything but. Behind the scenes is a deep, complex process that brings your voice and message to life.

A professional ghostwriter starts with in-depth interviews to understand your ideas and experiences. They work to capture the core message you want to communicate. They research your industry, analyze trends, and ensure the book is aligned with your goals. They create an outline that structures your book to flow logically, engage readers, and deliver impact.

The writing process isn't about stringing words together, it's about capturing your voice and reflecting your unique insights. Each chapter is carefully crafted, revised, and polished, sometimes rewritten multiple times, to ensure it's engaging, clear, and valuable.

The process can take anywhere from six months to a year, or longer, depending on the project's complexity. The skill and effort involved in professional ghostwriting explains why it costs between $.50 and $1.25 per word.

For a 60,000-word book, this translates to an investment ranging from $30,000 to $75,000. More experienced ghostwriters, especially those who specialize in high-level business books, memoirs, or technical subjects, can charge $100,000 or more. Celebrity ghostwriters, or those with a track record of bestsellers, often command $150,000+ per project.

Imagine this: You walk into a high-stakes meeting, and in your hands is your book, something that not only demonstrates your expertise but shows potential clients that you mean business. Your book isn't a tool; it's the key that unlocks new opportunities. With the right ghostwriter, that book can help you stand out in a crowded marketplace.

Ghostwriting isn't priced by the pound. It's about what your finished book can do, how it positions you, what doors it opens, and the way it elevates your credibility.

Return on Investment (ROI) – The Real Payoff

When you hire a ghostwriter, you're not paying for a manuscript, you're investing in a career-defining asset. Imagine this: You've poured months or even years of your life into creating a book. That book isn't a reflection of your ideas, but a powerful tool that opens doors, generates income, and solidifies your authority in your field.

Now, picture this: An investment of $30,000–$100,000 for a professionally crafted book is not a "one-time expense." It's the first step toward massive returns. How? A well-written book can help you secure speaking gigs that could earn you $10,000–$50,000 per engagement. It can position you as the go-to expert in your niche, making your expertise highly sought after by high-value clients.

> ROI isn't about what you spend upfront; it's about what your book will bring in long-term. The more strategic your book is, the higher the rewards it will yield.

Real-Life Examples of Success: Making Your Book Pay for Itself

Jane was initially hesitant to invest in a professional ghostwriter, questioning whether the cost would be worth it. But once she saw the outcome, she quickly realized the value. Her book, expertly crafted by her ghostwriter, didn't sit on a shelf, it became a powerful business asset.

Within six months, Jane closed over $300,000 in new contracts, directly attributed to the credibility her professionally written book gave her. The book positioned her as an authority, making her the go-to consultant for clients who saw her expertise in print. This wasn't luck; it was the result of investing in a high-quality book that worked as a lead magnet, trust-builder, and revenue generator.

Take another example: Connor, a seasoned business consultant, knew that to stand out in a saturated market, he needed something that set him apart. He hired a professional ghostwriter to create a book that showcased his innovative approach to scaling businesses.

Once published, Connor didn't send the book out for passive sales, but he strategically used it in every pitch, showing clients exactly how his methods could transform their businesses. Within three months, Connor secured $500,000 in new consulting contracts.

The book didn't pay for itself, it became an ongoing lead generator, helping him continue to land high-value clients long after the first round of sales. This success didn't happen by chance; it was the result of a professionally crafted book that directly contributed to his bottom line.

These aren't isolated cases. Investing in professional ghostwriting means investing in opportunities that will generate a far higher return than the initial cost. If your book is aligned with your business goals and executed well, it has the potential to open doors and make money long after it's published.

Time and Effort Saved – The Invisible Cost of Doing It Yourself

Consider the time and energy it takes to write a book: research, structure, editing, and revisions. If you're trying to do it yourself, you're not spending hours writing, you're spending weeks or months figuring it all out, managing the logistics, and likely getting stuck in a cycle of frustration.

Hiring a professional ghostwriter may seem expensive, but what you're gaining is time, time to stay focused on your business while the heavy lifting gets done behind the scenes. By hiring a skilled writer, you're freeing up your time to focus on what matters most: running your business, meeting clients, and pursuing other projects.

While a DIY book might save you a chunk of money upfront, you'll be spending hundreds of hours that could be better spent elsewhere. It's simple math: You're either paying now or paying later in terms of lost time and opportunity. Ghostwriters give you a product you don't have to wrestle with, and a final product that's of a higher quality than something you could produce on your own, even if you had the time.

The Hidden Cost of Hiring a Cheap Ghostwriter

Many people, trying to save money, turn to ghostwriters offering services for a few thousand dollars or less. On the surface, it seems like a great deal. But cheap ghostwriting almost always leads to disaster.

Imagine hiring the cheapest contractor to build your house. The structure might look fine at first glance, but over time, cracks appear, leaks form, and eventually, the whole thing falls apart. A cheap ghostwriter is like that contractor; they might deliver something that looks like a book, but when people start reading, the flaws become obvious.

Low-cost ghostwriters often lack experience, leading to disorganized, generic, or poorly written content. They don't take the time to capture your voice, which means your book sounds like a random compilation of thoughts rather than a well-crafted story. They rush through projects, often juggling multiple clients at once, and fail to give your book the attention it deserves.

Worst of all, many cheap ghostwriters don't even finish the job. They take on too many projects, realize they're in over their heads, and disappear halfway through.

Many authors who try to cut costs end up paying twice, once for a cheap ghostwriter who delivers a low-quality draft, and then again for a professional who has to rewrite the book from scratch.

It's natural to feel overwhelmed when starting the writing process. But remember, you don't have to do it alone. A good ghostwriter is here to guide you, taking the burden off your shoulders and helping you craft a story that will resonate with your audience.

What a Ghostwriter Does. And What They Don't

A professional ghostwriter takes your ideas and turns them into a polished, compelling book that sounds exactly like you. They guide you through the process, ensuring that your message is clear, your structure is strong, and your final product is professional.

But ghostwriters don't do everything.

Ghostwriters don't handle marketing and book promotion. If you want to make your book a bestseller, you'll need a marketing strategy. A ghostwriter's job is to create the book, not to sell it.

They don't manage publishing logistics. While some ghostwriters offer consulting on self-publishing, most won't handle things like ISBNs, cover design, or setting up your Amazon listing. Those tasks fall under publishing services, not writing.

And ghostwriters don't offer unlimited revisions. Most agreements include one or two rounds of revisions to refine the manuscript. If you decide mid-project that you want to take the book in an entirely different direction, that's not a revision, it's a rewrite, and it costs extra.

The Real Cost of Doing It Right vs. Doing It Twice

Many people hesitate at the cost of hiring a professional ghostwriter.

A well-executed book elevates your brand, attracts high-value clients, and positions you as an industry leader. It can land you speaking engagements, media opportunities, and business partnerships. It can be a lifelong asset that continues to open doors long after it's published.

A book that's done poorly, however, does the opposite. It makes you look unprofessional. It confuses readers instead of inspiring them. It fails to generate business, and worse, damages your reputation.

If your book is important to you, if you see it as a tool to build your career, share your expertise, and create long-term opportunities, then investing in quality isn't optional.

The difference between a $5,000 ghostwriter and a $75,000 one isn't price: it's the difference between forgettable and career-defining.

What's holding you back from writing your book? Take a moment to consider what a professionally written book could do for your business: client acquisition, speaking opportunities, or elevating your status as an expert. Now, let's make it happen.

Your Book Deserves to Be Done Right

If you're serious about publishing a book that reflects the best of what you have to offer, hiring a professional ghostwriter is one of the smartest investments you can make.

A great ghostwriter brings more than writing skills. They bring expertise, strategy, and the ability to tell your story in a way that not only engages readers but also positions you as an authority.

So, before you cut corners or settle for a low-cost option, ask yourself:

Do you want a book that exists? Or do you want a book that makes an impact?

Flexible Payment Options – Making Ghostwriting Work for You

A client I'll call Brendan came to me with a problem. He had a book idea that was genuinely good — a leadership framework he'd developed over twenty years that his coaching clients kept referencing back to. But Brendan was bootstrapping a second business and couldn't write a check for $45,000 in one shot. He assumed that meant the book wasn't happening.

It didn't. We structured it as four milestone payments tied to delivery stages. He paid when each phase landed, which meant he could fund it from revenue as the project moved forward. The book was finished in eight months. Brendan's story isn't unusual. Most ghostwriting arrangements have more flexibility than the sticker price implies.

While most ghostwriting arrangements are built on flat-fee pricing, some ghostwriters are open to alternative payment models, if the project has commercial potential and the author brings real assets to the table. This section explores a few of the most common alternatives, when they might work, and what to keep in mind if you're thinking of suggesting one.

Milestone or Installment Payments

A common milestone structure: 25% upon contract signing, 25% upon delivery of the outline, 25% upon delivery of the first draft, and 25% upon project completion.

Or, more simply, a down payment plus monthly installments.

This model benefits both sides. You, as the author, aren't writing a massive check all at once. Meanwhile, the ghostwriter receives steady compensation as the project moves forward. This arrangement also keeps everyone accountable and moving forward.

Royalties and Profit Sharing

This is the option most people ask about, but it's also the one least often accepted.

Royalty or profit-sharing arrangements are most viable when you have a large and engaged audience — an email list, podcast listeners, or active followers — a clear and documented promotion plan, a history of successful launches, and a book with business potential beyond royalties such as upselling services or products.

Professional ghostwriting is a paid craft, not a gamble on future book sales. While authors dream of big sales, most books don't sell more than a few hundred copies. Unless a project already has proven demand, relying solely on royalties is a financial risk most ghostwriters won't take.

Hybrid Models

If you can't afford a full flat fee but your book has clear commercial potential, some ghostwriters may offer a hybrid model - a reduced fee in exchange for a share of royalties or other revenue the book generates after launch.

Hybrid payment models work best when both parties are entrepreneurial and transparent, there's a high level of trust and communication, and the author has a clear, strategic plan to monetize the book.

Think of this like a partnership. You're both investing in the outcome, your ghostwriter with their time and expertise, and you with your network and marketing efforts. But make no mistake: this still requires a solid contract and a strong mutual understanding of expectations.

Why Royalty-Only Offers Are Usually Declined

Authors sometimes approach ghostwriters with ideas like, "I can't pay you now, but when the book sells, you'll get 50%." This is almost always a red flag.

Royalty-only offers are rarely accepted because ghostwriters can't control what happens after the manuscript is delivered, marketing and distribution are entirely out of their hands, and most books never generate enough in royalties to cover even a fraction of the work invested.

Ghostwriters aren't trying to shut down your idea, they're protecting their time and livelihood. Professional ghostwriters know their value, and they've seen too many well-meaning authors disappear after promising big returns that never come. If you're asking for a royalty-only model, you need to offer more than hope. You need a compelling plan.

Alternative Funding Ideas

Alternative funding paths worth exploring: if the book supports your business, treat it as a marketing expense. Crowdfunding platforms like Kickstarter or Indiegogo can raise funds before a word is written. And sponsorship is worth considering — could a company or strategic partner benefit from being associated with your book?

Don't rule yourself out because your budget is tight. With a little creativity, and the right mindset, you might be surprised by what's possible.

Final Thoughts: The Right Deal Is Built on Trust

The strongest ghostwriting relationships start with clear expectations, shared goals, and mutual respect, not numbers on a page. A flat fee may be standard, but flexibility exists when there's trust, professionalism, and a well-thought-out plan behind your book.

If you're hoping to explore a different payment structure, bring clarity, honesty, and value to the conversation. Come to the table prepared, respect their time and back up your vision with clear business potential and creative direction.

A great ghostwriter is a strategic partner, not someone taking a shot in the dark. When the arrangement works for both sides, everyone wins — and your book ends up in the hands of the readers who need it most.

Overcoming Challenges in the Ghostwriting Process

Joshua had always wanted to write a book. He was an accomplished entrepreneur with years of experience, and his story was one he knew could inspire others. He had valuable lessons to share about perseverance, growth, and leadership. But writing a book? That was a whole different ball game.

He had a clear vision of what the book would be: a guide for aspiring entrepreneurs to navigate the toughest parts of building a business. He wanted it to be inspirational, practical, and impactful. But as the days went by, Joshua realized that writing a book wasn't as simple as he thought.

Joshua underestimated the complexity. Outlining chapters, wrestling with tone, and finding his voice, all of it proved tougher than he imagined.

Managing Expectations: When the Vision Doesn't Match Reality

Joshua pictured his book in readers' hands during layovers and coffee breaks, something accessible yet impactful. He dreamed of sparking conversations, not sales.

However, when he began working with his ghostwriter, things started to feel more complicated than he expected. His initial vision was broad, maybe even a little too ambitious for the timeline they had set. He wanted to tackle a range of topics, from personal stories to business strategies, and wanted it all in a single book.

The ghostwriter, who had worked with other clients before, gently helped Joshua see that it would be difficult to fit so much into one book. The scope was too large. The ideas were amazing, but the book would need to focus more narrowly to be effective.

Joshua wasn't thrilled about it at first. He had spent years developing his ideas and wanted to fit as much as possible into the pages. However, with his ghostwriter's help, they took the time to refocus the project. Instead of trying to write a one-size-fits-all guide, they narrowed it down to the core message: lessons about overcoming early setbacks in business.

It wasn't easy, but Joshua saw that scaling back wasn't a defeat; it was strategy. By focusing on a single theme, he could go deeper and make a bigger impact.

Key Takeaway: A great book begins with clear expectations, about what you want to say, the impact you want to make, and the time and resources available to get it done.

Overcoming Writer's Block: When the Words Just Won't Come

A few weeks into the project, Joshua was feeling frustrated. He knew his message was important, but when he sat down to write, the words felt like they were trapped. His thoughts were scattered, and no matter how much he tried, he couldn't seem to get them onto paper in a meaningful way.

There was mounting pressure to get everything right. He had high expectations for himself and the book, but the fear of not delivering the perfect draft froze him. He found himself staring at a blank page, overwhelmed by the idea of creating something that was both professional and personal.

That's when his ghostwriter intervened again. She reassured him that the first draft didn't have to be perfect. Perfection wasn't the goal; progress was. She encouraged him to stop worrying about every little detail and start writing. The key was to get the words on the page, even if they weren't perfect.

Joshua finally took the advice to heart. He allowed himself to write freely, focusing less on perfection and more on expressing his ideas. Slowly but surely, the words began to flow.

Key Takeaway: Writer's block often stems from the pressure to be perfect. Allowing yourself to write freely without the fear of imperfection can get the creative process moving.

Handling Feedback: Navigating the Critique

When Joshua received the first draft, he was both excited and anxious. He knew it was only the beginning, but seeing his ideas on paper made it feel real. He was eager to see if his vision had come through.

But when he started reading through the draft, Joshua realized that it wasn't exactly what he had imagined. Some parts didn't capture his voice the way he wanted, and others needed more depth. There were even sections that didn't align with the tone he envisioned.

His first instinct was to take it personally. After all, these were his thoughts, his words, how could they not capture his voice?

But his ghostwriter helped him see it differently. She explained that this was a first draft, and it was only the starting point. Feedback and revisions were part of the process, and she would work closely with him to ensure the final manuscript sounded exactly the way he wanted.

Joshua learned that feedback wasn't criticism of him as a person; it was a tool to make the book better. He and his ghostwriter worked together to refine the content and make sure every word aligned with the message he wanted to send.

Key Takeaway: Feedback is essential for improving your work. Use it as an opportunity to refine your ideas and make the book even stronger.

Navigating Disagreements: When the Vision Changes Mid-Project

About halfway through the writing process, Joshua started to have second thoughts. As he worked on the book, he realized that he didn't want to speak to entrepreneurs anymore, he wanted the book to appeal to a wider audience. He wanted it to resonate with anyone who was struggling, regardless of their business background.

This shift in vision caused some tension. They had already spent a lot of time working on the structure, focusing on business owners. Changing the direction of the book mid-course could potentially delay everything.

But instead of letting frustration take over, Joshua had an open conversation with his ghostwriter. They discussed how they could adapt the content to be more inclusive without losing the core of the message. Together, they brainstormed ways to incorporate universal themes of perseverance and overcoming challenges that would speak to a broader audience.

The project wasn't derailed, it was elevated. Joshua learned that flexibility and open communication with his ghostwriter could help him create a book that was more aligned with his evolving vision.

Key Takeaway: Be open to adjusting your vision, especially if you feel it will make the book better. A good ghostwriter will help you navigate changes without losing sight of the book's core message.

Final Thoughts: Embracing the Process

Despite the challenges — managing expectations, overcoming writer's block, handling feedback, and navigating shifts in vision — Joshua's book was finally complete. It was everything he had dreamed it would be: personal, authentic, and full of actionable advice. The process had been long and filled with moments of doubt, but it had also been incredibly rewarding.

Joshua realized that writing a book wasn't a linear process. It was a journey that required collaboration, patience, and a willingness to adjust along the way. His ghostwriter had helped him at every step, guiding him through the tough moments, offering support during times of uncertainty, and helping him shape his ideas into something powerful.

In the end, Joshua understood that the challenges were not setbacks, they were opportunities to improve, refine, and create a book that truly reflected his vision and voice.

Beyond the Book: Other Creative Paths for Your Story

Not every idea fits neatly into the format of a traditional book. Sometimes, the story in your head has more visual impact.

Sometimes, your concept leans more toward dialogue than narrative. And sometimes—let's be honest—you're more drawn to a movie deal than a bookstore shelf.

There's nothing wrong with that.

In fact, many aspiring authors overlook alternative formats that may serve their ideas even better than a standard nonfiction book or novel. This chapter explores other powerful storytelling formats—from screenplays to short story anthologies—and the real-world implications of choosing one of those paths.

Why It Matters

Choosing the right format isn't just a creative decision, it's a strategic one. The structure you choose affects everything: how long it takes to produce, what kind of collaborators you need, how much it costs, and what kind of return you can expect.

Let's look at the main options beyond books.

Screenplays: Writing for Film or Streaming

Some stories scream to be seen.

If your idea is cinematic—full of action, suspense, fast dialogue, or vivid scenes, a screenplay might be the right fit.

But screenwriting is its own beast. It follows strict formatting rules, a different pace of storytelling, and an entirely different business model. It's not about internal monologue or long exposition; it's about what the audience can see and hear.

A screenplay needs a compelling concept with strong visual moments, dialogue that carries most of the weight, and a clear three-act structure — which is almost mandatory in film.

Ramifications: You may need a writing partner, especially if you're more of a storyteller than a screenwriter. And be ready—Hollywood is crowded, and getting noticed usually means working through agents, contests, or networking events.

Stage Plays: Writing for the Theater

If your story thrives on character interaction, tension, and limited settings, a stage play might bring it to life in a whole new way. Theater is intimate. It thrives on dialogue, character conflict, and emotional highs.

A stage play typically focuses on a few central characters, takes place in one to three key locations, and relies heavily on powerful dialogue and stage direction.

Think of stories where the drama comes from what's said and unsaid, not car chases and visual spectacle.

Ramifications: If you want to see your work produced, you'll need connections in the theater world—or be ready to self-produce. Small local theaters often accept submissions or host new writer nights.

Short Story Collections

Maybe you don't have a single 50,000-word idea. Maybe you have ten 5,000-word ones.

Short story collections work well for writers who enjoy experimenting with different styles or voices, concepts that pack a punch without requiring a full book, and testing ideas before committing to novel-length work.

This format works well for speculative fiction, slice-of-life memoirs, and even business parables. It's also a way to build a brand if you want to release themed collections around a topic or genre.

Ramifications: Collections are harder to sell unless you already have a following. But they're fast to produce, easy to serialize online, and great for building an author platform.

Hybrid Works: Books That Could Be More

Some stories lend themselves to formats beyond the book entirely: a documentary, a podcast series, a scripted YouTube series, or a serialized Substack or blog.

This path opens up new opportunities—but it also adds complexity. You may need more collaborators, more funding, and a longer lead time.

Real Example: *Hidden Valley Road* and the Power of a True Story

In 2020, Robert Kolker published *Hidden Valley Road*, a nonfiction book about a Colorado family with twelve children—six of whom were diagnosed with schizophrenia. The story, rooted in real-life trauma, science, and family resilience, was originally pitched as a deeply reported book.

But the power of the narrative didn't stop on the page.

Before long, *Hidden Valley Road* was optioned for film. The story's emotional weight and complex characters caught the attention of studios looking for dramatic, character-driven adaptations. Oprah selected it for her book club, and soon after, the rights were sold for a potential series or feature-length film.

Kolker's work started as a book—but its impact was bigger than print. It became part of a cultural conversation about mental illness, family secrets, and the line between science and story.

> *Some true stories are too vivid, too dramatic, and too layered to stay confined to one format. The right book can launch a multi-platform presence—if it's told well from the start.*

So, What's the "Right" Path?

The right path depends on your strengths as a storyteller, your target audience, and your long-term goals.

Ask yourself: do you want readers, viewers, or listeners? Are you after impact, credibility, or entertainment? And do you want to sell copies, option rights, or attract media attention?

Your story might deserve a book. But it might also deserve a stage. Or a screen. Or a stream.

Whatever it is, don't limit yourself.

Ghostwriting Fiction: Why It's Harder Than You Think (and Why It's Worth It)

Writing fiction is personal. It's also intimidating.

Whether it's the novel that's lived in your head for years, or a story you started and stopped a dozen times, getting it out of your imagination and onto the page is a lot harder than it seems.

You might have characters whispering in your ear, a plot that won't leave you alone, or an entire world you've been building in your mind for years. But when you sit down to write? Everything goes quiet.

That's where ghostwriting comes in.

Not as a shortcut. Not as a cheat code.

But as a collaborative process that helps you bring your vision to life, without spending the next five years frustrated, stuck, or questioning whether your story was ever worth telling.

You Have the Story. So Why Haven't You Written It?

Nathan had always been a storyteller. As a kid, he invented worlds with plastic dinosaurs and pirate ships. As an adult, his storytelling became more refined; presentations that moved clients, speeches that made people cry. But when it came to writing his novel, he hit a wall.

For years, Nathan had dreamed of publishing a science fiction epic. He had maps, character arcs, handwritten notes, and even playlists for each major scene. But no matter how many times he tried to write it, he never got past the first few pages.

He wasn't lazy. He wasn't undisciplined.

He was just stuck.

And like many aspiring authors, Nathan ran headfirst into three invisible barriers that stop fiction writers in their tracks.

Barrier #1: "I Know the Story in My Head, But I Can't Get It on the Page."

Nathan knew his characters better than some of his real-life friends. He could explain the political system of his imaginary world down to the tax code. But when it came time to write the opening chapter?

Blank screen.

He'd write a few lines, then delete them. Rewrite. Backspace. Rewrite again.

Nothing sounded like what he saw in his mind.

The deeper issue wasn't a lack of creativity, it was translation. Turning imagination into prose takes a different skillset. And every time Nathan couldn't bridge the gap, he lost momentum.

Barrier #2: "I Don't Know Where to Start… or Stop."

Should he start with the dramatic flashback or the present-day storyline?

Should the villain's origin come early or be revealed later?

Was this one book or a trilogy?

Nathan was drowning in options. Every choice felt like the wrong one. And without structure, he couldn't move forward.

He'd read advice blogs, taken webinars, even tried writing software that promised to solve everything. But what he really needed was a second brain, a creative partner who could help untangle the mess and build something solid.

Barrier #3: "I Don't Want to Lose My Voice."

Nathan was a storyteller. This was *his* story.

The last thing he wanted was for someone else to write it in a way that didn't sound like him. He worried that if he brought in a ghostwriter, the final result would be flat, generic, or worse—unrecognizable.

He'd read books before where the author's name felt like a lie.

So, he hesitated. He waited. And with every passing month, the story he'd been carrying stayed locked inside him, waiting for the moment he'd finally act.

The Turning Point: From Frustration to a Finished Book

Instead of asking Nathan for a fully polished outline, the ghostwriter started with a conversation.

They talked through characters. Backstories. Tone. Pacing. What Nathan wanted readers to *feel* when they hit certain scenes.

Then the ghostwriter built a sample chapter to show what was possible—and it sounded exactly like Nathan. Only better. Cleaner. More alive.

From there, they worked together.

Nathan stayed deeply involved, guiding the emotional beats, the dialogue, the themes. But he wasn't stuck anymore. He was building momentum—with someone who understood the craft of fiction and respected the soul of his story.

Six months later, he had a completed manuscript in hand.

Not a shadow of his idea. *His* idea—realized.

What Happens If You Don't Get Help?

Nathan almost gave up on his book.

And if he had, the story he'd carried for decades would still be locked inside his head. Nobody would've ever met the characters he loved, or seen the world he built.

But when he stopped trying to do it alone, everything moved faster.

The draft got done. The story came to life. And for the first time, Nathan didn't just *dream* about being a novelist—he *was* one.

Do Ghostwriters Write Fiction?

One of the questions I hear all the time is, *"Can ghostwriters do fiction?"*

And the answer is: absolutely.

If you've got a story you want to tell—whether it's a love story, a spy thriller, or a cosmic war spanning galaxies—chances are, a ghostwriter can help bring it to life.

Here's what most people don't realize: fiction ghostwriting isn't just about stringing words together. It's about capturing voice, building momentum, keeping characters consistent, and making sure the pacing hits just right. You're not hiring someone to write for you, you're hiring someone to co-create with you. To help you tell the story that's been trapped in your head for far too long.

Some clients show up with detailed character backstories and three-ring binders full of worldbuilding. Others just have a vibe— "It's kind of like *Stranger Things* meets *Bridgerton*, but with pirates." That's more than enough to start.

The range of fiction I've helped bring to life is wider than most people expect. A sci-fi founder came to me with nothing but a short story he'd written ten years earlier, and together we turned it into a five-book space opera series. A retired executive with no writing background hired a ghostwriter to tell a historical romance set in 1920s Harlem, loosely inspired by her grandmother's letters. And a therapist who wanted to explore themes of grief and healing through a novel worked with a ghostwriter to create a beautiful, character-driven coming-of-age story she now gives to clients.

The truth is, it doesn't matter what your genre is, what matters is the emotional truth behind it. If your story matters to you, a good ghostwriter can help make it matter to readers too.

Whether you're working on a thriller, a romance, a fantasy saga, or something genre-bending that doesn't fit a single category, you don't have to do it alone. With the right partner, fiction becomes a shared creative journey— one where your ideas finally make it to the page.

What Kind of Fiction Can Be Ghostwritten?

One of the biggest misconceptions is that ghostwriting only works for memoirs, business books, or nonfiction.

Not true.

Fiction ghostwriting is alive and well—and it spans every genre you can imagine. Whether you're building galaxies or crafting love stories, a great ghostwriter can help you bring that vision to life.

Some clients come in with pages of character sketches and a fleshed-out universe. Others have nothing more than a loose idea and a "what if..." scenario. Either can work.

Science Fiction & Fantasy, Thrillers & Crime Novels, Romance & Relationship-Driven Fiction, Historical Fiction, Literary Fiction, Adventure & Coming-of-Age, and Hybrid or Genre-Bending works — all of these can be ghostwritten.

You've got worldbuilding, intricate systems, alien languages, and magic rules that need to make sense. Ghostwriters help keep everything grounded, consistent, and compelling—without info-dumping or losing emotional depth.

These books rely on tight plotting and precise pacing. If your story has twists, murders, cops, detectives, or conspiracies, a ghostwriter can help structure the suspense and keep readers turning pages.

Whether it's steamy, sweet, or somewhere in between, romance depends on emotional arcs and believable connection. Ghostwriters know how to write chemistry, character growth, and page-turning tension.

Want to set your story in 14th-century France or during the Harlem Renaissance? Ghostwriters help with research, accuracy, and staying true to the voice and mood of the era—while keeping the story readable.

If your book leans more lyrical, symbolic, or thematic, ghostwriters can work closely with you to preserve the nuance and make sure your style shines through.

Stories about personal growth, travel, transformation, or survival—these often need balance between emotion, action, and reflection. A ghostwriter can help you thread it all together.

Have a sci-fi romance thriller set in the Victorian era with talking cats? Cool. A seasoned ghostwriter will help you stitch it all into something that works on the page, even if it sounds wild out loud.

If you have a story that doesn't fit neatly into a genre, that's okay. Most great fiction blends elements anyway. What matters is the emotional truth of your story—and a good ghostwriter knows how to protect that while building structure and style around it.

Ghostwriting Memoir: Telling Your Story Without Losing Your Voice

Memoirs are not the same as autobiography. It's not just a list of what happened, and it's not meant to include every detail of your life. Memoir is about meaning—a specific slice of your life, told with emotional honesty, insight, and a clear narrative arc. It's the "why it matters" behind the "what happened."

But here's the thing most people don't realize until they try to write one: telling your own story is hard. Much harder than it seems.

You're not just recalling facts. You're deciding which parts of your life are worth sharing. You're reentering moments that might still be raw. You're navigating what to say—and what to leave out—when people you love might read it. You're trying to write something meaningful, something powerful, something that does justice to what you've lived through... and often, the words don't come.

That's where a ghostwriter can help.

Why Memoir Writers Get Stuck

Most memoirs never get finished. Not because people don't have stories worth telling—but because of three barriers that stop them cold:

Barrier #1: Emotional Overload

It's one thing to *remember* what happened. It's another to relive it while trying to write it down. Clients often say, "I thought I had dealt with this... but writing it brought it all back." A good ghostwriter becomes part storyteller, part therapist—creating a safe space where you can talk through your memories, even the painful ones, and know they'll be handled with care.

Barrier #2: Narrative Chaos

Life doesn't happen in neat arcs or tidy chapters. It's messy. Memoir isn't about recording everything—it's about selecting the moments that tell a larger truth. Most people struggle with scope. "Should I start with my childhood? Should I tell the story of my business? My marriage? The time I got sober?" A ghostwriter helps you find the central theme and structure it in a way that flows like a novel—clear, compelling, and emotionally powerful.

Barrier #3: Self-Censorship

Memoir requires vulnerability. That's terrifying.

People worry about offending family, exposing secrets, or being judged. They second-guess themselves. They write a few chapters, then hide them in a drawer.

A ghostwriter doesn't just write your story, they help you *own* it. You get to decide what's included: what's private, and what's said in between the lines.

Real Story: Frank's Memoir Nearly Broke Him—Then He Got Help

Frank was a retired firefighter. After decades of service, he had more stories than most people live in five lifetimes—heroism, grief, PTSD, even a near-death experience. His wife had begged him to write it all down, and he tried. But every time he sat down to write, the memories came rushing back too hard, too fast.

He wrote two chapters, then deleted them.

When we started working together, Frank told me he didn't want to "make it a sob story." He wanted to honor his crew, talk about resilience, and pass on what he'd learned the hard way. Over several interviews, we unpacked the highs and lows—on his terms. I asked the hard questions when needed, gave him space when things got heavy, and together we created a manuscript that was brave, grounded, and utterly him.

The result? Not just a book. A legacy. Frank's grandkids now know the man behind the badge. His story is being used in firefighter training programs. He finally said what he needed to say—and did it without retraumatizing himself or giving up control.

What Types of Memoirs Can a Ghostwriter Help With?

Memoirs aren't just for celebrities and politicians. Some of the most moving books come from everyday people who've lived through extraordinary things. If you've ever thought, *someone needs to hear this,* you might be right.

Ghostwriters help with survival and recovery stories — overcoming trauma, addiction, illness, or abuse; legacy memoirs written for children, grandchildren, or community; faith journeys and stories of spiritual transformation; immigrant and identity stories navigating life between cultures; business memoirs chronicling rags-to-riches journeys or hard leadership lessons; love and loss memoirs about relationships, grief, divorce, or reconciliation; and turning-point memoirs focused on a single decision or season that changed everything.

A ghostwriter helps you clarify the focus, organize the structure, and bring your story to life with empathy, precision, and voice. Your voice.

But Is It Still *Your* Memoir?

Yes.

Ghostwriting doesn't take away ownership. It brings clarity to your story and gives it the shape it needs to move other people. You're still the author. Your name goes on the cover. You're just bringing in a professional to help do justice to something too important to leave unfinished.

If you've ever said, *I need to write this down,* then your story already matters. The question is: will you tell it while you still can?

Conclusion: What's Your Next Step?

Most people never finish their book. You did. That puts you in a category that most professionals only talk about from the outside. What happens next depends entirely on what you do with it.

Whatever brought you to this point — building credibility, leaving a legacy, attracting clients, or finally saying something you've carried for years — that reason is still real. The book exists now. The question is what you do with it.

Hiding your book doesn't shortchange your brand, it holds back the people who could learn from your experience. Every great leader, coach, and entrepreneur has a story worth telling. The ones who succeed? They share it.

Now, it's your turn.

I started writing at 17, sitting across from my grandfather as he described surviving the Bataan Death March. I didn't know then that I'd spend the rest of my life helping people tell the stories that matter most. But I know now that every book I've helped create — every memoir, every business book, every novel that finally made it off the kitchen table — started with someone deciding their story was worth telling. So does yours.

What Happens on Our First Call

If you're ready to have a conversation, here's what to expect. We schedule 30 minutes. No pitch, no pressure. I'll ask you three questions: what do you want the book to do for you, who are you writing it for, and what's stopped you from starting until now.

That's it. From those three questions I can usually tell you whether ghostwriting is the right path, what kind of book makes sense, and roughly what the process would look like. Some people leave the call with a clear direction and do it themselves. Others decide they want a partner. Either way, you'll know more than you do now.

The call is free. The clarity is the point.

Book a call now at https://contact.thewritingking.com

You've got something to say. Let's make sure the world hears it.

About the Author

Richard Lowe didn't always know he would become a ghostwriter. For years, he built a thriving career in the tech world, serving as the Director of Computer Operations at Trader Joe's. He managed thousands of systems, led digital transformation initiatives, and handled everything from cybersecurity to disaster recovery. From the outside, it looked like success. Inside, though, something was missing.

That missing piece had been with him since childhood. As a teenager, Richard interviewed his grandfather, a World War II veteran who survived the Bataan Death March. He turned those stories into a short book, not for profit or praise, but because he knew those memories mattered. He had a deep respect for history and an instinct for capturing the heart of a story. That early project planted the seed for what would eventually become a second career—one built around helping others tell their own powerful truths.

After years in corporate leadership, Richard made a bold decision. He walked away from the stability and stress of the tech world to pursue his real passion: writing. With no backup plan and only his savings, he moved to Florida, joined a ghostwriting firm, and quickly realized he could go further on his own. Within three days of leaving that job, he had $25,000 in client projects lined up. That was over a decade ago. Since then, he has never looked back.

Today, Richard is one of the most experienced ghostwriters working in the field. He has written or ghostwritten more than 100 books for clients across every imaginable industry. His work includes memoirs, business books, thought leadership platforms, fiction, and coaching guides. He's written for executives, doctors, scientists, artists, and everyday people who have lived extraordinary lives.

What sets Richard apart is his ability to truly listen. His background in leadership taught him how to navigate complexity, and his natural empathy allows him to uncover the emotional core of a story. His clients often say the same thing: *"You captured my voice better than I ever could."* That's not a formula. That's the result of patience, intuition, and a commitment to making sure every book sounds like the person who lived it.

Outside of writing, Richard's life is full of unexpected adventures. He once photographed over 1,200 dance performances, building strong friendships with performers from all walks of life. He hosted elaborate birthday parties that brought together hundreds of dancers and artists. He took up photography not just as a creative outlet, but as a way to connect with people and document beauty in motion. That same attention to detail and sense of wonder carries into his work as a ghostwriter.

Richard has also written science fiction, taught young people how to protect themselves online, and helped clients turn painful divorces, career pivots, and quiet victories into books that inspire and heal. Some of his ghostwritten projects have led to keynote speeches, media coverage, business deals, and even international recognition. More importantly, his books have helped people feel seen, heard, and understood.

His process is straightforward. He works closely with each client, asking deep questions, recording thoughtful interviews, and guiding them through every step of the journey. Whether they're a first-time author or a seasoned entrepreneur, he meets them where they are and brings out their best ideas with honesty and care. For Richard, ghostwriting isn't just a service. It's a partnership.

Clients trust him because he keeps their voice at the center. He never imposes his own agenda. He's not trying to sound clever or use trendy phrases. His goal is simple: to help people create books they can be proud of. Books that sound like them, read like conversations, and move readers to action.

Richard also mentors up-and-coming writers, speaks on podcasts, and contributes to thought leadership circles. He continues to run his own business and develop new resources for professionals who want to share their stories but don't know where to start.

He currently lives in Florida, where he enjoys early mornings, quiet walks, and deep conversations. He is a lifelong learner and a quiet observer, always listening for the story beneath the surface. You won't find him chasing attention. You'll find him building something lasting, one conversation at a time.

To learn more about Richard's ghostwriting and book coaching services, visit TheWritingKing.com or connect with him on LinkedIn at Richard Lowe. Whether you have a book idea or just the feeling that your story matters, Richard is ready to help you bring it to life.

Richard's books are available at masterofworlds.com. For free publishing insights and industry updates, visit thewritingking.substack.com. For ghostwriting and book coaching services, see thewritingking.com.

Acknowledgements

Writing a book is never a solo journey, and I am deeply grateful to the incredible people who walked beside me.

First, heartfelt thanks to my sister, Belinda Lowe-Schmahl, and her family. Your love and encouragement have meant everything. Belinda's work with Schmahl Science Workshops has inspired countless young minds, including mine. (Learn more about her mission at https://schmahlscience.org/mission)

To my grandfather, Frank Hoeffer, a true American hero. As a young man, he served with honor in World War II—surviving the Bataan Death March, enduring years as a prisoner of war in Japan, and returning home with quiet strength and deep humility. He rarely spoke of what he endured, but his courage shaped our family and inspired my earliest sense of what it means to leave a legacy. Interviewing him as a teenager became the first book I ever wrote, and in many ways, it sparked this lifelong calling. Thank you, Grandpa, for your sacrifice, your spirit, and your example.

To Lola, my childhood friend with the rock and cactus collection, who taught me the value of friendship long before I understood its weight. Your presence in my early years was a gift, and your curiosity and kindness left a lasting imprint on who I became.

To Zeya, Sasha, and Aubrey: three extraordinary women whose kindness, strength, and willingness to listen made all the difference when life got heavy. In the moments I needed support the most, you were there with open hearts and wise words. Thank you for being steady, compassionate presences in my life.

To Steve Davis, my mentor at Software Techniques Inc., thank you for teaching me how to think bigger, lead smarter, and grow with integrity. Your mentorship helped shape not only my professional path but also my belief in what's possible. (Learn more about Steve: https://www.linkedin.com/in/stevedavistechnology/)

To Jimmy James, whose wisdom, energy, and constant encouragement have been a source of motivation throughout this journey. Your belief in my work, and in me, has made a bigger difference than you probably realize. Thank you for being a true ally and champion.

To Royce "The Writer", a brilliant creative and generous spirit. Thank you for being a thoughtful sounding board, a talented writer in your own right, and an example of what it means to elevate the craft. (Connect with him here: https://www.linkedin.com/in/royce-the-writer/)

To John Shields (deceased), former CEO of Trader Joe's and Macy's, thank you for showing me what true leadership looks like. You were the first (and only) leader in a corporate setting to treat me with genuine respect, and that left a lasting mark on my life. Your integrity, vision, and humanity continue to inspire the way I lead and serve others today.

To my old friend Dan Milan, guitarist, technologist, storyteller, and soul of humor and wisdom. Back when music meant wires, amps, and gut-driven blues, you were always chasing the real sound. Your letter from Salt Lake, half guitar confessional, half-life update, still makes me smile. From mountain winters and MIDI rigs to stories of fearsome foursomes and dogs that outrank bosses, you brought richness to my life through honesty, music, and memory. You always knew how to make a small moment big. I hope we reconnect someday and pick up right where we left off—mid-song, mid-joke, mid-dream.

A huge thank you to David Cogan and the entire Eliances community. Eliances is more than a network, it's a force. Eliances.com is an online hub for entrepreneurs, offering connection, collaboration, and support. From resources and interviews to live Q&As, Eliances helps keep the entrepreneurial spirit alive. You've helped push me forward when I needed it most.

To some of my best friends from the bellydance world: Mardhavi Sakuntala, Erika Barrus, Marjhani, Jamilla, Sherri Wheatley, Deanna Hallum, Ayse Cerami, Tonantzin Bolaños, Nancy Wallace, Mi-Ri El Khoury, Elizabeth Souza, Devilla Raks, Faizeh Al-Zarqa, Gigi Corkett, Heather Shoopman, Kristina Nekyia Cañizares, Leilainia Marcus, Michelle Hilario, Kaotar Dee, Nilay Engin, Olu Nicole, Polly Paulina Carey, Pleasant Gehman, Rachel Rene George, Rita Blaik, Sarah Al Nour, Seylena Troi, Shirin Raqs, Frances Ratonel, Alia Saeed, Perizad Christine, Aubre Hill, April Rose, Mardhavi Sakuntala, Sabrina Fox, Sabrina Moyes, Sooz, Jenny Aguilar-Mikkelsen, Christina Rizkallah, and Edenia Archuleta. Thank you for the joy, movement, and energy you've brought into my life. Whether through performance, collaboration, or friendship, each of you helped shape a vibrant chapter of my journey.

My friends at the Renaissance Festivals including Willie Banger, David Wine, Adam Reid, and the members of The Gentlemen Adventurers, Babu Ku, The Merry Wives of Windsor, Poxy Boggards, Pye Powder Court, Danse Macabre, The Fantastikals, The Puritans, The Queens Court, and the Yeoman of the Queen's Guard. You were there for me, although you may not have realized it, during the tough times when my wife passed away.

To my brilliant tattoo artist, Roni Zulu, and my creative, loyal friends Donavon Lerman, Lee Corkett, Adam Reid, Lewis Vern (deceased), and Robert (Lopaka) Souza: thank you for being with me through transformation, self-expression, and unapologetic reinvention.

To Mick Foley, WWE legend, comedian, and bestselling author: thank you for showing the world that storytelling, vulnerability, and strength are not opposites. Your example as a writer and performer has been a genuine inspiration in how I approach storytelling, humor, and heart.

This book stands on the shoulders of each of you. I'm honored to walk this path with such extraordinary people.

Books by Richard Lowe

See books by Richard Lowe at

https://masterofworlds.com

Get free publishing insights and industry updates at

https://thewritingking.substack.com

For ghostwriting and book coaching services see

https://thewritingking.com